OUR HIGHER POWER
Accessing Your Divine Gifts

By:

David Starr and Francesca Rose

COPYRIGHT

Copyright © 2024 by David Starr and Francesca Rose

All rights reserved. No part of this publication may be reproduced, distributed, or transmitted in any form or by any means, including photocopying, recording, or other electronic or mechanical methods, without the prior written permission of the publisher, except in the case of brief quotations embodied in critical reviews and certain other noncommercial uses permitted by copyright law. For permission requests, write to the publisher at the address below

This book is a work of nonfiction. While the authors have made every effort to ensure the accuracy and completeness of the information contained herein, they assume no responsibility for errors or omissions. Any perceived slights of specific people or organizations are unintentional.

ISBN: 979-8-9915522-0-2

Published by David Starr and Francesca Rose

First Edition

DEDICATION

We dedicate this book to our children for their patience as we spent countless hours assisting others and engaging in spiritual practices to align with our source selves in the hopes of cultivating world peace. May our words find you and help you magnetize the overflowing gifts of the divine.

TABLE OF CONTENT

Dedication 2

Foreword 3

Acknowledgements 7

Chapter 1: Creating Sacred Space 12

Chapter 2: Clearing, Purifying, and Centering Yourself 20

Chapter 3: Sourcing Spiritual Cleansing and Hygiene 28

Chapter 4: How to Ground and Anchor Your Gifts 46

Chapter 5: Accessing Your Akashic Records 56

Chapter 6: The First Gift Activation 62

Chapter 7: The Second Gift Activation 74

Chapter 8: The Third Gift Activation 84

Chapter 9: The Fourth Gift Activation 98

Chapter 10: Visiting the Realms. 112

Chapter 11: Creating Spiritual Activations. 124

Chapter 12: Hieros Gamos. 142

Chapter 13: Higher Self Communication. 154

Chapter 14: The Gift of Sight, Astral Projection, and Astral Travel. . . .

. . . . 166

Chapter 15: Individual Readings. 182

Chapter 16: Land Clearing 194

Chapter 17: Automatic Writing. 204

Chapter 18: Activating Clairs. 212

Chapter 19: Grid Work. 228

Chapter 20: Reconnecting Your Heart to the All. 234

Conclusion 240

About the Authors 244

Francesca Rose. 246

AUTHOR'S NOTE

Welcome, and thank you for accompanying us, David and Francesca, on our inner space travels. Together, we will guide you on a soul journey to energetically expand into your best spiritual gifts. You don't need a ship to explore space; your body is a ship, and by using your consciousness, you can energetically travel anywhere in the Omniverse.

There are those living life on auto-pilot, and there are those of us harnessing our source energy, evolving the world a little more each day. If you have come across this book, you are one of those people tapping into your higher power. Magnetizing this information will uncover the hidden treasures that exist inside of you.

In this book, we will teach new metaphysical techniques that will align you with your spiritual gifts and help you become one with the divine that exists within. Our goal is to help resurrect the pure source energy inside of us all so that we may shift in consciousness together, sharing our unlimited spiritual gifts as one big soul family.

Power to the heart. Let there be light.

ACKNOWLEDGEMENTS

A special "I love you" to our family and soul family for their endless faith and support. We love you tremendously. We especially want to thank our soul sister, Katie Lorah, for keeping us organized and on task. Her editing efforts were divine and went above and beyond anything we could have hoped. We would also Like to Thank Bonnie Burd, Tan Gail and Yvonne Gatez for their testimonies.

FOREWORD

Your Higher Power begins by guiding readers through essential practices like creating sacred space and spiritual hygiene, laying a strong foundation for deeper spiritual exploration. As the book unfolds, it delves into advanced practices such as channeling, accessing Akashic Records, and performing land clearing, offering readers both mystical experiences and practical tools that they can integrate into their daily lives.

The feedback we've received highlights the profound impact this book has on its readers. Tannis Legary, a reader deeply engaged in spiritual practices, shared:

"David Starr and Francesca Rose have crafted a book that I could not put down! As I read, I felt a transformative shift within myself, leading to a new way of thinking. With insightful practical exercises, spiritual wisdom, and personal stories, the authors create a compassionate and encouraging tone, providing a safe space for readers to explore their spiritual journey and connect with their higher selves."

Yvonne Ganetz, another dedicated practitioner, expressed how the book helped elevate her spiritual practices to new heights:

"I always channel every day, but now with all the activations, something happened. I could feel my channelings reach a new, higher level, and I started channeling realms that I hadn't channeled before."

Bonnie Burd, a Wellness Practitioner and Reiki Master, emphasized that:

"*Your Higher Power* is more than a book—it is a spiritual companion, a guide that lovingly walks beside you as you explore the vastness of your spiritual potential."

INTRODUCTION

We have entered a new era on Earth. Since industrialization and the advent of worldwide globalization, technological advancements have emphasized consumption, manipulation, and the unequal distribution of wealth among an elite few. As the global population surpasses 10 billion, the need for natural resources has thrown Mother Gaia out of alignment, with deforestation facilitating the infrastructure required for the rapidly growing population.

In a world built on the ideals of money, power, and acceleration, many people look outside of themselves to discover their place and their peace through monetary freedom. Ironically, those who achieve the most financial freedom are often left feeling incomplete and dissatisfied, with an unsettling desire to consume more to fill the void within.

During the COVID-19 lockdowns, a confusing time, most were forced to stay in their homes. The home workplace environment became (and still is) a leading trend as big corporations downsized and the value of home life increased. During this time, many began to ask questions like, "What is the truth? Why am I here? There has to be more to life."

These questions led to an awakening on Gaia. Many souls have realized that there is more to life than just earning and consuming, working and sleeping, and blindly following the American Dream when something inside them is saying, "There is more."

This pattern of thought evolved into a consciousness shift of awareness. Many are now feeling and sensing that deep within them exists a soul—a being perfect in love, living in an imperfect world of fear, division, control, and manipulation. As the next root race of humanity forms their consciousness, they align with being part of God, an eternal being, a being of love above the imperfect conditions imposed by those who regulate and commercialize people, places, and culture.

Welcome to the New Age. We are nearing a tipping point in humanity's new consciousness evolution. As more individuals find this inner power, they become the power, the freedom, and the embodiment of the dream of love.

This is the purpose of your Higher Power: to begin learning to access your God-given gifts and come into your highest divinity.

CHAPTER 1
CREATING SACRED SPACE

Sacred spaces have been a part of human culture for thousands of years. Ancient civilizations such as the Egyptians, Mayans, and Greeks built temples and altars to honor and worship their gods and connect with the divine. These spaces were often aligned with celestial bodies, emphasizing their connection to the cosmos.

Sacred spaces were not only places of worship but also places of healing and community gatherings. For example, Native American medicine wheels were used for spiritual ceremonies and healing practices, while European stone circles, like Stonehenge, were believed to be centers of astronomical and spiritual significance.

With this understanding, we invite you into the most beautiful energies in the Omniverse by creating your sacred space. The act of creating sacred space is a personal journey, a ritual that holds sacred power. Sacred space is not just a physical manifestation but a way of living—a holistic approach to nourishing the mind, body, and soul with vibrations of the highest order. It's akin to enveloping oneself and others in a glowing bubble of the purest light, a space where all spiritual practices find solace and magnificence.

Every day, we honor this practice with reverence, inspired by the wisdom passed down by the enlightened ones. Treating our bodies as sacred temples is not merely a duty but a profound responsibility. Creating sacred space transcends mere ritual; it intertwines with our existence, shaping our interactions and guiding us to radiate the most exquisite energies to those around us. As teachers of divine evolution, sacred space is our anchor, grounding us and paving the way for the purest transmissions of divine light. Whether performed at the beginning of one of our Master Classes or during an individual reading, the sanctity of this space sets the tone, ensuring comfort and receptivity among participants.

In this holy space, one can customize the experience, with the vibration of crystals and the aroma of sage, that the dance of energy unfolds, weaving a tapestry of healing and enlightenment for all involved. The fabric of sacred space extends beyond physical boundaries—it is a beacon of intention, a fortress of light in a realm where energies converge. Within this sphere of protection and illumination, we commune with the most sacred entities—angels, guides, elementals, ancestors—conjuring their presence to infuse sessions with profound wisdom and grace.

Creating sacred space isn't merely a series of rituals; it's a profound act of setting intentions and aligning with the highest good. Clearing stagnant energies with the purifying smoke of sage, we breathe in the essence of transformation. The crystals, with their silent hum, elevate the vibrational frequency, casting a shimmering veil of light around us. Through the sound of creation—Om—our spirit ascends, resonating with the cosmic power of the Trinity. Grounding ourselves, we envision roots of light spiraling into the earth, anchoring us to the heartbeat of Gaia, while also connecting us to the celestial realms above. As you can see, the ritual of grounding, of calling in the sacred energies, is not just a ceremony but a communion—a sacred dialogue with the universe.

Sacred space is also about boundaries—a sacred boundary that shields us from discordant energies and welcomes only the purest vibrations of love and light. It's about intention, about wielding the potent tool of light to forge connections, to heal, to ascend. In this space of creation, where colors of light intermingle and dance, where golden threads of purity weave through the fabric of reality, we find ourselves immersed in a symphony of cosmic energies, resonating with the very essence of creation itself. This chapter isn't just about creating sacred space; it's about embodying it, living it, and breathing it into every facet of our being. It's a journey of self-discovery, a voyage into the heart of the divine, where the sacred and the mundane converge, gifting us with a tapestry of transcendent experiences and a gateway to our highest light.

Integrating the power of spoken words enhances the sanctity of the space further. Using verbalized affirmations such as, "Only the highest vibrations of love are welcomed in my sacred space" or "I align with my higher self for divine guidance" adds layers of intention and resonance to the sacred environment.

Creating Sacred Space with Golden Light

A great way to create sacred space is by working with golden light. With intention, you can draw in the radiant energy from the golden source and guide it with your hands to form a luminous circle around you. The rhythmic expansion of this golden light as you move, synchronized with each breath, creates a protective and vibrant aura. Following this, purify the space by drawing in pure light from your higher self. Focus on the energy cleansing the sacred space through intentional breathwork.

Crystal Grids in Sacred Spaces

It can be helpful to create a crystal grid around your sacred space. Crystals amplify your intentions. As you create a sacred space, the crystals amplify those intentions and energy. Additionally, the crystals work as anchor points for light. Much like a column supporting a building structure, a crystal holds a light column. These light columns make up the fortress and walls of your sacred space.

Francesca creates sacred space for her writings, readings, and Omnigoddess master class to ensure only the purest source light energy comes in. Sacred space makes the energy beautiful and secure for all parties involved. She creates an intuitive crystal grid for each class based on the collective energy of the participants. The powerful crystal arrangement brings a variety of vibrations that circulate natural divinity in crystal form around the room. Some crystals clear, ground, amplify, or bring otherworldly vibrations. Crystal grids add a wonderful ambiance to any spiritual situation you are guided to use them for.

During one of David's visits to Mount Shasta, where he first connected with Telos, the Lemurian crystal city under the mountain, the Telosians told him how to create a very special crystal grid that he still uses today.

The Telos Crystal Grid

It is important to have a crystal in every direction (N, S, E, W) and at every corner (NE, NW, SE, SW), forming a circular pattern. Then, it is essential to have a pointed crystal in the true North position pointing up towards the heavens and a pointed crystal in the true South position pointing down towards inner Earth. You may need to find something to prop the South crystal so it stays in position. Once this formation is completed, you will begin to connect your heart energy to the crystals.

First, connect your heart energy to the crystals at true North and true South by breathing into your heart and exhaling love to those points. Then, connect your heart to true East and true West by breathing into your heart and exhaling love into those crystals. Spend a moment really feeling and becoming aware of the connection to true North, South, East, and West. After you feel this energy, intend to expand this field to encompass the entire circular formation. You will feel a massive energy expansion. This process creates one of the strongest higher-energy crystal grid sacred spaces that you can have. It's the perfect energy for astral traveling or receiving messages from your higher self. Some may ask, "What type of crystals should I use?" The best answer is to use the ones you are intuitively called and guided to use.

Once you have created your sacred space, join us in this guided meditation:

- Close your eyes and breathe into your heart, then exhale into your sacred space.

- Call in your guide teams, Angel guides, Higher Self, and Mother Father God.

- Ask to receive divine messages to assist you on your path of ascension and spiritual journey.

- Sit in the energy and begin to become aware of your angel guides or Mother Father God. You may feel the love energy grow even more.

- Listen with your heart to the messages, images, or words they bring.

- When you are done, always thank the divine for their messages. Gratitude is a must.

Sacred Space Through Other Advanced Rituals and Practices

Seasonal and Lunar Rituals:

Celebrate the solstices and equinoxes with specific rituals, such as lighting candles to honor the return of the sun during the winter solstice. Engage in lunar rituals like setting new moon intentions and performing full moon release ceremonies to align with the natural cycles.

Incorporating Movement and Sound:

Incorporate movement and sound into your spiritual practices by using drumming to raise energy, chanting mantras to focus the mind, and dancing to embody spiritual intentions. These practices can enhance your connection to the divine and deepen your spiritual experience.

Psychological and Emotional Benefits

Reducing Stress and Improving Mental Health:

Studies show that having a designated sacred space can provide a sense of peace and sanctuary, reducing anxiety and promoting relaxation. Personal testimonies highlight how daily meditation in a sacred space can enhance emotional resilience and mental clarity.

Supporting Emotional Healing:

The ideas are only limited to your imagination. Support your emotional healing by journaling in your sacred space, practicing gratitude rituals, and using visualization to release negative emotions and invite positive energy. These techniques can help you process emotions and cultivate a more positive outlook.

gratitude rituals, and using visualization to release negative emotions and invite positive energy. These techniques can help you process emotions and cultivate a more positive outlook.

CHAPTER 2
CLEARING, PURIFYING, AND CENTERING YOURSELF
Preparing the Vessel for Gift Activation

In this chapter, we delve into the essence of priming by focusing on clearing, purifying, and centering oneself as a prelude to activating your inherent spiritual gifts. This process involves harnessing the light to cleanse and purify not just your personal energy field but also the energy of your surroundings. This type of cleansing serves as an alternative method to smudging, ensuring a pristine energetic environment.

Connecting with the Golden Light

When we cleanse our energy fields, our preferred approach involves the power of breath. We connect with the golden light through each breath—inhaling its purity, flooding our sacred space with it, purifying our clients, and establishing a profound connection with our higher selves. The most potent practice in this purifying ritual involves connecting to one's higher self through one's "pillar of light."

The Pillar of Light

The pillar of light serves as your divine conduit, a connection originating from above, streaming through your head, and grounding into Mother Earth. To activate your pillar of light:

Take a breath of the surrounding golden light, drawing it into your crown chakra as you inhale.

With intent, guide it down to your heart and exhale, sending it through your lower chakras and into the heart of Mother Earth.

On the subsequent breath, inhale the crystalline energies of Mother Earth through your feet or Earth Star chakra, channeling it up to your Solar Plexus chakra.

As you exhale, disperse it out through your crown to connect with your higher self, all the while maintaining a clear intention.

This process solidifies your link to source and your divine essence, allowing you to seek guidance and insight from your higher self. It serves as a profound tool, particularly beneficial when navigating significant life decisions, as it offers divine support along your path.

God Commands

Another potent method of clearing involves the use of "God commands." As one awakens to their true power, entities of density may persist, especially during vulnerable moments such as sleep. Have you ever experienced a nightmare? It could likely be a manifestation of these density beings.

One effective God command involves invoking the presence of Mother Father Prime Creator. By stating, "I call on Mother Father Prime Creator to cleanse and clear my fields, protect my energy during rest, purify my living space, and guide all that contravenes universal law into the light. Thank you," you not only establish a shield of protection but also express gratitude to the divine forces. Remember, gratitude is a powerful force, as the divine entities only seek appreciation in return. Therefore, it is integral to convey your thanks consistently.

Grounding and Priming

A pivotal practice interwoven into all spiritual endeavors is the act of connecting to the source essence while simultaneously grounding oneself. Priming signifies delving into a mental space wherein the connection to the prime creator is tangibly felt, known, and observed, safeguarding oneself from the influence of illusory energies.

An effective and comprehensive priming ritual is anchoring oneself from below, from above, and all-encompassing. Begin with grounding as a foundational step. A visualization technique for grounding involves growing roots of light from the feet that extend deep into Gaia's soul, wrapping around her 111 times. Symbolic of wishes, the 111 wraps imbue intention and codes for the desired gift activation, drawing the pure Gaia gift code upwards through the body to the source level. Witnessing the unwrapping of the spiritual gift at the source level instills a profound sense of awareness and support, enshrining the new gift within every facet of life and existence.

The Power of Intention

For those less visual, the same outcome can be attained through pure-hearted intentions, as the potent power of intentions has the ability to propel one into the chosen energy realm. Once the intention is sincerely expressed, unlocking any spiritual gift becomes achievable, guided by the purity of intention and heart-driven motivation.

By surrendering one's vessel to divine utilization for the greater good, an intriguing mystical secret unfolds—an instantaneous activation of cherished spiritual gifts within oneself. This process necessitates a genuine commitment, as it entails a soul vow to embody a collective energy channel, offering assistance to all in alignment with divine will.

Energy Exchange and Oracle Decks

Another accessible method involves an energy exchange through seeking service from a gift activator. By reciprocating this energy exchange, one receives the frequency of the gift, unlocking its manifestation within oneself. Emphasizing the unique nature of each gift, sharing and exchanging one's gifts not only expands their dimensions but also promotes an elevated collective vibration and consciousness expansion.

Leveraging tools like activated oracle decks crafted by way showers also holds significant value in unlocking spiritual gifts. Recognizing the importance of monetary exchange as a form of appreciation for the effort and energy invested in creating these transformative resources, one can view it as a form of spiritual personal training, enriching the journey of spiritual growth and collective evolution.

Daily Energy Clearing

Complementing the activation of spiritual gifts is delving into the significance of clearing energy to experience the highest joy in life. Adopting a daily practice of clearing energy by fostering a mindset of positivity and happiness proves to be transformative. Acknowledging and releasing negative energies by escorting them into the light for purification initiates a cleansing process, bridging profound connections with the energies flowing through oneself and fostering a deeper understanding of one's internal dialogue.

Nature's Purification

In exploring the potent energy purification offered by nature, tree-hugging emerges as a sacred exchange of energies, enabling the transmutation of negativity into positive vibrations, mirroring the trees' ability to cleanse the environment. Additionally, tapping into Dragon energetic medicine allows the release of negative energies by invoking the image of a dragon breathing the violet flame upon oneself.

Conclusion

Everyone and everything is a divine reflection of the source energy animating the all. By using the above techniques, you will quantumly reprogram the wrong thinking of separation in your mind, which helps to embrace the realization that you are an unlimited source being undergoing a human experience. A profound sense of preparation unfolds for navigating life's experiences. Cultivating a perspective of interconnectedness and shared creator energy, this chapter underscores the transformative power of recognizing the inherent unity among all beings, invoking a deep-seated understanding of collective support and mutual assistance.

An exercise for balancing and aligning your chakras

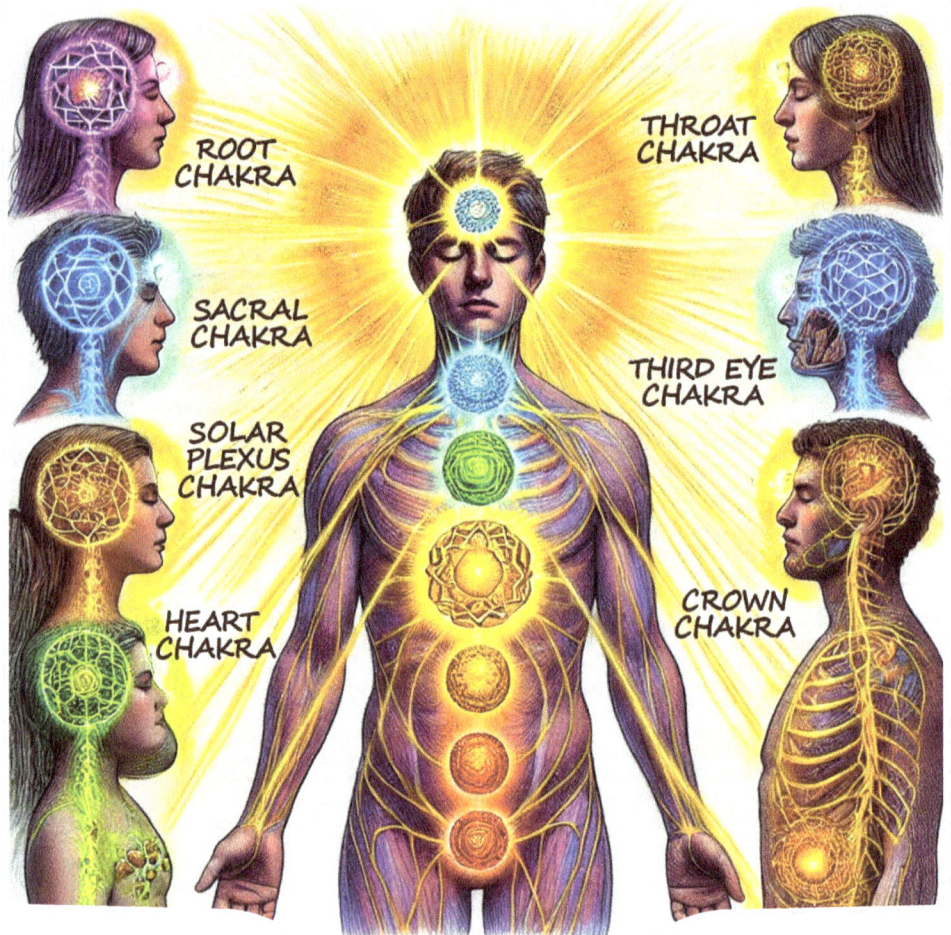

Step 1. Breathe golden light into your third eye chakra from the middle of the forehead to the back of your head, clearing and aligning (with intention) your third eye chakra.

Step 2. Breathe golden light into your throat chakra from the front of the throat to the back of the throat, clearing and aligning your throat chakra and aligning it to your third eye chakra.

Step 3. Breathe golden light into your heart chakra from the front of the heart to the back of the heart, clearing and aligning it to your throat and third eye chakras.

Step 4. Breathe golden light into your solar plexus chakra from the front of the solar plexus to the back of the solar plexus, clearing and aligning it to your heart, throat, and third eye chakras.

Step 5. Breathe golden light into your sacral chakra from the front of the sacral to the back of the sacral, clearing and aligning it to your solar plexus, heart, throat, and third eye chakras.

Step 6. Breathe golden light into your root chakra, clearing and aligning it to your sacral, solar plexus, heart, throat, and third eye chakras.

Step 7. Breathe golden light into your crown chakra, clearing and aligning it to your third eye, throat, heart, solar plexus, and sacral chakras, and exhaling the golden light out your root chakra, connecting and grounding it into the heart of Mother Earth.

Step 8. Sit and focus your intentions on all your chakras coming into balance, becoming aware of the peace and tranquility in your energy.

CHAPTER 3
SOURCING SPIRITUAL CLEANSING AND HYGIENE

Sourcing Spiritual Cleansing and Hygiene

Spiritual hygiene involves practices and rituals to cleanse, balance, and align your energy, promoting overall well-being and spiritual growth. Techniques include breathwork, using elemental energies, and grounding exercises that intentionally create light. Visualizations and intention setting help focus and amplify these efforts. Incorporating these practices can reduce stress, support emotional healing, and enhance mental clarity.

By creating a sacred space and integrating modern tools like the violet flame you can maintain a high-vibrational environment that fosters peace, resilience, and spiritual connection. Spiritual cleansing is a routine you can develop on your own; it is like a shower for the soul, cleansing your energetic field so the best energies align with you and course through your day. Spiritual cleansing involves daily practices that make the soul feel good and keep you on your highest timeline path to your source consciousness evolution. The whole collective on this planet has been preparing for this jump in evolution, whether they are aware of it or not.

When you develop your spiritual tool belt, the whole ascension process becomes easier. Everybody can tap into and navigate this Earth structure through much higher vibrational energies that we all carry and hold within, contrasted with staying in the false energy constructs built around us through societal conditioning. These false constructs place filters over our experiences to reflect agendas that prevent us from witnessing our full source connection. Like an onion, we must peel away all the false layers covering our full light of pure source awareness.

Similarly, our light is veiled by this illusory programming that we bought into due to our belief to blindly accept everything we were taught by family traditions and society. When the blind lead the blind, we do not go far in expanding our consciousness. That's where sourcing comes in—returning to our purity of pure source energy. We do this by healing our energetic wounds, pulling out false conditioning, and replacing it with the highest light of truth.

Routines to Build Your Spiritual Arsenal

Starting your day by expressing gratitude for all you are thankful for launches you instantly into the heavenly realms of self. Gratitude is a vibration that reaches the most divine version of yourself and acts as an automatic feedback mechanism, sending back more of what you are truly grateful for into your life. Gratitude can transform your day into a beautiful one. When you feel grateful throughout the day, embrace and amplify that energy by sitting in it and enjoying it as long as possible. Gratitude has the energetic frequency that makes dreams come true. The frequency of gratitude is incredibly powerful.

Setting intentions for your day and keeping them as a central focus will magnetize what your heart desires into your reality. Your focused thoughts are your magic wand. What you focus your thoughts on is your highest currency. What you truly believe in with every ounce of your heart energy shows up in your current reality. When you align with the divine and witness what you want as already created in the source realm, your nonphysical source energy effortlessly molds your three-dimensional experiences into the reality of your dreams.

When you stay focused on the highest expectations for yourself, your nonphysical source energy will grant your wishes through source alignment. What you expect matches the creational power of your source self. When you stay aligned with the frequency of the highest peace within, you will be in a steady creational flow of purified source energy.

Including activities you love throughout your day amplifies your vibration to optimal levels. In this way, you can raise your conscious awareness to match the heart of the divine. Don't just live for the moment—live for joy moments that match the soul of the divine. Activities like walking the dog, enjoying Mother Nature and her organic gifts, hanging out with the kids, meditating, writing, and helping others find Source within are perfect examples of how we, too, bask in our joy. When you follow your bliss, you multiply your blessings.

One can take any moment and turn it into a spiritual practice that expands the light quotient surfacing onto the Earth from within your soul. When driving, you can bless people on the road, sending Source energy and protection to everyone. The intention of sending love alchemizes any situation into a positive one. Sending love to the birds, the flowers, the trees, and everyone in the world is a magical prayer that blesses your life tenfold.

When you stand in a line, you can connect with others' higher selves through visualization or intention and exchange energetic Source code. Spirituality is supposed to be fun, and you can customize your metaphysical practices to what makes your heart feel good. We highly recommend connecting to your inner child for guidance in turning mundane life activities into a game. Doing the things we love is the key to unlimited joy creation.

Forming a relationship with your guides makes your life much easier. Because we have free will, you must ask your guides for help. They are always waiting patiently to answer your call. The most secure way to receive messages from your highest light guides is to ask the highest source energy to send any guides or guidance that will help make your life more blissful. When you do this, messages and guidance will show up in different ways through the people and the world around you. You simply need to keep an open mind and an open heart to receive divine energy and transmissions.

You have free will, so you can ask for the highest light to come in and assist you. If you don't know how to start your spiritual process, a dragon, angel, fairy, ancestor, or an ascended master will be appointed to you to guide you. Whatever type of guide reflects your highest timeline path will show up. You can call on the energy that feels safe and loving to you. The good thing is that you have been all things in the Omni-dimensional realms, so your guides are just energy streaming through you from other dimensions. Don't be scared—it is just you guiding you.

Through repetition, spiritual best practices evolve and become second nature. When you are in positive energies and experiencing positive feelings, you are in divine energy. Continue using the tools you develop that aid you in feeling good.

One way to do shadow work is to use "violet rain" with intention or visualization. Imagine violet rain falling on you with ease and grace. As it falls, your traumas and hurts will come forward to be cleared. To clear the trauma, welcome it and ask what it did for you and what it is trying to tell you. You must also forgive yourself and all parties involved, knowing that every lesson has a blessing involved, whether you can see it or not. By doing this process, you send all the trauma into the light to be recycled as a higher source energy. Energy cannot be destroyed, but we can transform it into an evolved form that recycles back to us and serves our evolution into our highest creational light.

Clearing the collective while invoking the thought of God in every word and every song is another powerful tool. For example, instead of "Love is a Battlefield," imagine "Love is peace." God is peace. The more you think of God, the more peace you will embody. The more you include the thought of God in everything, the more your body will release all stored pain and stress from this lifetime and all lifetimes. The thought of God burns away all false illusions instantly because the thought of God instantly connects you to the frequency of the highest light of truth. We created every line of this book with God in mind, so it serves as a source activation in each word.

Energetic Cords and the Violet Flame

Energetic cords form when someone connects to you energetically. Energetic cords can occur for many different reasons, such as fights, someone acting as though they are superior to you, making fun of you, talking behind your back, being angry at you, or desiring to be with you intimately. Knowing these techniques is essential for managing such connections. Our favorite metaphysical modality to assist with density removal caused by cords is the violet flame. This amazing technique was brought into this world by Saint Germaine.

David and Francesca both share St. Germaine as one of their guides. David has received extensive training with Saint Germaine in the etheric realms for many years and has always been one of his primary guides. Saint Germaine taught David how he obtained the violet flame and how to use it properly. It is excellent at clearing trauma and removing cords and is easy to use.

Using the violet flame is all about intention and visualization. It's important to know you have two major chakras in the palms of your hands. These chakras are where you intentionally create the violet flame. Visualize it like a little violet fire growing in the palm of your hand. Then intend for that violet fire to grow larger and larger over your hands until it encompasses your arms, your head, and your entire body. Everywhere the violet flame touches, it purifies your light and clears away the energetic cords.

It's that easy--when you get into a fight, violet flame yourself. When you walk into a big space, violet flame yourself. Why? Because other people can give you energetic viruses or their negative energy. Have you ever passed someone and suddenly felt off? That's their negative energy getting into your field. Use the violet flame right away to transmute it.

David recalls one day waking up feeling like a million dollars. As he got in the car to drive to work that morning, he suddenly felt angry and upset. He intuitively knew this negativity wasn't coming from him. As he looked at the car passing him, he noticed the man was in a state of rage, yelling and upset. David knew instantly the reason he felt angry was he had picked up the other driver's negative energy. As a result, David used the violet flame on his energy field. As soon as he did, the negativity cleared away and he felt like a million bucks again.

Francesca also uses violet flame instantly when she feels any anxiety. She simply thinks of the word violet flame, and the density is transmuted. The more you work with this modality, the stronger it becomes in you. With practice, the results will amaze you. It is quantum soul medicine.

Inner Child Healing

One of the most important healings you can embark on is to heal the trauma from your childhood. Inner child healing will lead to shadow work, the quickest way to raise your vibration and come into the love frequency to shift your consciousness and belief systems.

What is inner child healing? It is healing your inner childhood wounds. When you reflect, you can rediscover your most hurtful childhood memories. Some have received abuse, verbal, physical, sexual, and neglect, to name a few. These childhood experiences harm the heart and cause our inner child to hide. As we get older, we forget we buried this trauma, which is likely the cause of our insecurities, negative self-image, and lack of confidence.

The common denominator for most people is they did not get the love they needed to feel fully nurtured as a child. So where is this child hiding? In your heart, behind secret doors you have locked and sent into the abyss of suppression. It is important to open the doors where your inner child is hiding and let them know you are ready to heal him/her.

Once you intend to open those doors, send healing golden light into all the areas the inner child is hiding in. Ask the angels to assist you in healing the child's heart. Forgive parents, siblings, school bullies, etc., whoever caused your younger self heartache, pain, despair, anger, or sadness for not giving you the love you needed. Then send healing from your heart to your inner child in all the situations they suffered. This is a rescue mission of your true essence before all the wounding occurred to bring you back into source alignment.

When this process is over, you must intend to pull the inner child out of all those hiding spaces and love and embrace him/her. With intention, hug your inner child and let your inner child know it's safe and that you will ensure you live your life full of joy now that your inner child is free. Then, let the adventure begin. Inner child healing work will bring you great peace, joy, and happiness. Your vibration will shift. Your beliefs will begin to change, and you will start to love yourself, your life, and your moments. Eureka!

What a breakthrough.

Shadow Work

Inner child healing is the gateway to shadow work. Some refer to shadow work as "inner work" because as you change your inner reality, your outer reality changes, too. The inner work journey is the most rewarding because as your vibration changes, so do your belief systems. One by one, you let go of old patterns, negative thoughts, karmic loops, and insecurities. You come into self-love, the love frequency, and a higher version of yourself until one day, you can truly say you love yourself and have enough.

Regarding David's one-on-one sessions, he states, "I do shadow work for my clients. I can literally see the darkest cords and looping patterns that the client needs to clear. As I share with the clients what I see and feel regarding their past lifetimes, every client tells me I am describing their current life. Why? It is because unhealed past lives or past life experiences create density loops and karma loops in your current lifetime, and until you heal them you repeat those loops. When those past lives and past life experiences are healed, you no longer live through those loops. Shadow work can transform your life: abusive relationships can turn into divine relationships, betrayals in partnerships become trusting partnerships, and narcissistic relationships become supportive relationships." Some call David the expert in the field of shadow work as he created what is possibly the first course on the planet on shadow work called "Embodiment of a Master."

Shadow work can save your life. One of the biggest causes of disease is density within. David states, "I will never forget when I received a text message from a friend who said their friend was dying in a hospital. They had been throwing up for 3 days straight and had no life force energy left. The doctors were unable to diagnose the issue. They came to me because of my supernatural gifts. I tuned into the man and connected to my divine teams, who told me his deceased father was trying to merge with him because they shared a dark past life that needed to be cleared, but the merging wasn't working. So, I asked the friend who texted me to find out if the man's father was around him. She said, 'Yes, his father has been around him the past few days.' Then, I went into this past life. After clearing this lifetime for about half an hour, I knew the patient would be ok. I told her he was going to be fine now. She couldn't believe it as he immediately stopped being sick and his vitals returned instantly. The doctor was also amazed and released him from the hospital within a few hours. About 1 year later, I had a vision dream where an angel brought me to this patient and his two kids in the woods. I saw him in his astral body. He flew over, gave me a hug, and said 'Thank you for saving my life.' The angel said more people will get sick if they don't do this inner work. This is why I spent the following 6 months creating the 'Embodiment of a Master' course."

Francesca also uses shadow work techniques in her Omni-Goddess Master Classes, as integrating your shadow is essential to aligning with the pure source energy inside yourself and all. We grow when we heal our traumas and rewrite our past stories from the lessons of how transmuting the darkness uncovered our hidden pockets of source light. To fully heal we need to understand our wounding and what this energy really is. We, as a collective, have so many hidden layers of societal conditioning and wounding we have repressed so far down that it festers our inner kingdoms and surfaces as repetitive negative emotions, loops, patterns, and situations in our current now moments. These unhealed traumas that live in our unconscious mind lower our vibration.

A perfect example is when we are in a sad mood. The sadness spreads to everyone we encounter like a plague. The negative emotion of sadness stems from an attachment to your original wounding. The wound keeps surfacing when inner turmoil from stressful situations matches the vibration of the original wound. Because the original wound was pushed away and not healed it took residence within your human. The wound will keep showing up because all wounds occur to teach you a lesson in duality and wish to be cleared and alchemized back into their original light form. You clear the wound when you witness the original wound and consciously release it by embracing your purity before the wound occurred, and then you integrate the lessons the wound taught you.

Wounding offers contrast in the dualistic world we are currently experiencing. Healing wounds expands our dimensions of self, giving us a greater appreciation of the light that we truly are. We can then use the experience from our wounding to create with the higher love appreciation that the healed energy of the wound expanded in us. Each healed wound will contribute to your character growth and further plug you into your original wholeness in your full source light. Until we come into full unity within the source collective on this Earth we are all a part of, we will continue to experience wounding within the concept that we are separated from God/Source and will continue to experience this dualistic contrast.

Without judgment, it is understood we are all at different levels of healing. However, it must be understood that the more one heals the self, the more the way is paved for collective healing in unity. It is so important in life to give everyone grace, including yourself. We build strength in our source light when we don't blame, make accusations, or speak against each other. We must continue the healing journey knowing we are in it together. This is not just one man's or one woman's journey; it is the journey of the collective consciousness that needs to be fully healed for all to find divinity in their relationships, love for self, and their lives. For all to live in equality, unity, and compassion for one another, we need to rise as a collective consciousness.

The concept of shadow work is simple. Find a wound or trauma, zero in on the vibration of it, then release it. To release the density within, you must use the power of forgiveness. We have both always loved the ancient Hawaiian tradition of Ho'oponopono. Ho'oponopono is an ancient Hawaiian practice of reconciliation and forgiveness. The term translates to "to make right" or "to correct." This spiritual practice involves a simple yet profound method of cleansing and healing oneself through the power of repentance, forgiveness, gratitude, and love.

The traditional Ho'oponopono practice involves a healer guiding individuals through a process of acknowledging and releasing negative emotions, thoughts, and memories that cause imbalance and disharmony. Modern adaptations of Ho'oponopono, popularized by Dr. Ihaleakala Hew Len, emphasize personal responsibility and self-healing. This approach involves repeating the four key phrases: "I'm sorry, please forgive me, thank you, I love you."

By continually expressing these sentiments, practitioners aim to cleanse themselves of negative energy, restore inner peace, and improve relationships with others. Ho'oponopono teaches that healing begins within oneself and that by healing our inner world, we can positively influence the outer world.

Shadow work is like Ho'oponopono, except it is more structured to focus on the underlying issues that plague your mind, emotions, and soul. It focuses on the very fabric of density that keeps people stuck in the cycles of karma and Earth. It is the most rewarding work because it's the only work you can take with you in the afterlife. When you start releasing the trauma of this life you can literally get hooked on healing yourself. It's all about healing, all the way to your full source light, and the vibration of what you want will show up in your reality as corresponding life pictures.

But there is a catch. You can do too much shadow work. How much is too much shadow work? Do not do shadow work if you are depressed as it can make you more depressed. Feeling depressed is a good indicator you are doing too much shadow work. David recalls asking Father God why he was showing David all these lifetimes where David was doing bad things as it was very depressing. Father God said, "It's because you keep asking to see these lifetimes. Seek and you shall find." David started asking to see good lifetimes, and as soon as he did, he saw a wonderful Atlantean past life where he learned how to create a crystal portal machine. David then took that past life memory to recreate the portal device, and it worked. How amazing! Past life work can feel good, too.

Francesca used shadow work to explore parts of her soul covered by a layer of hidden trauma buried so deeply in the hidden dimension of herself that it caused anxiety issues. As she did more shadow work, it opened a connection to her higher light guides and strengthened her connection to God/Source inside. She was able to heal her anxiety and connect many other people with tools to do the same. A stronger source connection makes it easier to open and unwrap your spiritual gifts and amplify and expand the dimensions of all that is good in your life.

Three golden rules to shadow work

- Stop if you are feeling depressed and do not start again until you are feeling 100% amazing.

- Do not do it more than two hours a week.

- Ask the angels to send you "pick-me-up" love energies after you do a session.

The angelic "pick-me-up" is key, because you go from feeling low to feeling love energy, and that's exactly what you need after this deep work.

In shadow work, there are victims and perpetrators. The perpetrators are the ones causing the trauma, and the victims are the receivers of it. There is also revenge backlash, where the victim becomes a participating perpetrator by projecting the perpetrator's trauma to someone else. In essence, the victim becomes the sole perpetrator.

If you ever retaliated or did bad things to others after they did them to you, you must also forgive yourself for re-projecting the trauma onto others. You need to send healing from your heart to the younger version of yourself to heal it fully and clear it once and for all. You will find you are less angry, your heart opens, and you have more joy, and if you start projecting, you will realize, "Hey, this isn't me anymore." The quality of your relationships with yourself and your family will improve.

Once you clear your childhood trauma, move on to your teenage years and adulthood. Go all the way up to your current moment, forgiving those who acted meanly, rudely, or abused you in any way. Send healing from your heart to these younger versions of yourself. Forgive yourself for any retaliation and re-projecting, and send healing from your heart to your heart back then. This technique dissolves the karmic cords between you and the people who hurt you. Once you go through your life examples like this and do this deep inner work, call on the angels to boost you with love energy. This process can be sad, and the healing can make you feel a little depressed as it releases out of you, so the angels are there to give you a boost and bring you back up.

To get this boost, call on the Archangels to come down and fill you up with golden light. This step is important to both get boosted up and to fill the void left by the density you cleared. This technique is how you shift your vibration and come into self-love the fastest. It's how you change your belief systems because you stop being the victim or the perpetrator and begin to see everything as a blessing that brought you into this now moment. This is when life starts to get magical.

Calling Back Your Power

Lastly, in shadow work, call back your power. Once you've completed the technique above, say, "I call back my power and light from everyone who took it from me. I give back anything I took from others. I call back my light from all timelines, dimensions, and realities to be with me now, cleansed, cleared, and healed." Once you do this, you will feel your energy come back. It's also good to do this when you wake up if you feel drained. As source beings with our nonphysical energy existing in Omni-dimensions, we do the craziest things when we sleep and we can deplete ourselves. Calling back your light replenishes it all.

A beautiful exercise to boost your love frequency:

Step 1. Place one hand over your heart and breathe love into your heart.

Step 2. With the other hand, your palm facing away from you, exhale the love into your energy field.

Step 3. Keep repeating and this will boost any low moods into tranquil, peaceful, loving ones.

CHAPTER 4
HOW TO GROUND AND ANCHOR YOUR GIFTS

Every human body is the temple of God/Source energy animating all. Knowing this should empower you to leap inside your consciousness and command the energetic gifts waiting to be witnessed and used for the greatest good of all. This is our birthright when taking human form, but no one told you this until now. We are currently amid a consciousness expansion, returning to the zero point of our source light. Our evolutionary growth is beyond grand. We can tap into the highest heaven and download energetic codes, information, and modalities from there or any world, dimension, or reality. We are Omni-dimensional beings, currently in our human awareness, housing all inside the source beingness that gives a pulse to all. We are all one God/Source energy, interconnected and woven like a spider web with all that has life.

We can tap into, receive, and send these energetic codes like magic, quantumly, for ourselves or share them with whomever we want, watching as they show up instantly in our life pictures. The same goes for spiritual gifts: we can share energetic codes or download them on our own from any realm, world, dimension, or reality. There is a whole invisible reality visible to those with their third eye open, and we will show you how to unlock your unlimited gift potential. But first, we need to highlight the importance of grounding.

Why Grounding is Important

When you ascend in consciousness, you become brighter and take on more light. Higher consciousness fields come to you to integrate into your energy. Therefore, it's important to know how to integrate them. Breathe in, inhaling the energies through the crown and all the chakras, and exhale them out through the soles of your feet into Gaia. Without grounding the ascension energies with this practice, you could end up with vertigo and dizziness as the energies linger on your crown chakra, waiting to be integrated.

Other great ways to ground include walking outside barefoot (be sure to stay away from glass or sharp stones and sticks) and hugging a tree. These techniques take you from the higher consciousness and return you to your body to remain connected with Mother Gaia. It is important to have higher consciousness experiences, but since you are living on Earth, after spending time in the higher chakras and higher consciousness, you need to come back down into the body to anchor the higher realm's energy into the Earth. When you ground, miracles from the energy you received during inter-dimensional journeys will manifest in your world because grounding is the most vital step in integrating energies from different dimensions and realms onto this Earth. Walking in nature and touching bushes and trees are all great ways to ground. When you are grounded, you anchor your light and integrate higher energies, which expand your gifts.

We came to this Earth to evolve our Omni-energetic repertoire. We need to learn how to better enjoy, expand, and utilize our human form in the now reality and infuse our energy with the energy of Earth. That is the starting point for activating spiritual gifts.

Grounding helps bring into reality the lessons of the subconscious mind from all our travels throughout our soul's journeys that are held within the subconscious mind. Grounding is the only way to integrate and download our gifts and masteries into the conscious mind. Our minds work like the iCloud system, housing all, and we, like cell phones, need to download what we want to view and experience on our life screen. By choosing with our intention and attention what we want to bring into focus at the forefront of our mind and life, our attention, intention, and action form the required formula for bringing spiritual gifts and all our dreams to life.

When we are not grounded, we accrue more information and store it in the subconscious mind where our Omni non-physical energy retains all information we encounter. When we ground ourselves and remain in the now moment as long as possible, we process the information and download it to the forefront of our minds, coming into union with it. By grounding in the present, the most important lessons will crystallize and manifest the experiences our souls wish to have in our Earth movie, where we are all stars.

Grounding with the Earth Star Chakra

The earth star chakra in your energetic center, located in your feet, is so powerful it instantly connects you to your energetic star Akashic Records that hold the birth and life charts of your soul signature. In our energetic blueprints, we house our pre-birth plan found in our star akashic records, formed when we first became rays of source light. Your soul signature can be described as originating when you were part of source, in wholeness. Imagine the source as a sun; this image gives you a visual representation of source in its wholeness.

Source energy then decided to venture out and explore, evolving into a sun ray or source ray, while still always remaining connected to the source. The impact of the source evolution into rays created a star, which is the first form. Stars house your soul signature journey from origin birth to all your soul signature travels, your different evolutions, journeys, and creations as a source ray of the source sun. The records of all these experiences are in the source sun, uploaded by each source ray as we expand and evolve into the newness and freshness of new creational energies.

In the now, we co-create with the source within, the next part of the movie consciously when we purposely put our thoughts of what we want into grounded action, instead of running on autopilot and floating unconsciously in different dimensions of our minds. When we are not grounded and exist in an uneventful, auto-pilot, default journey mode, life passes us by.

When we decide to ground, focus, and act on what we want every day, we awaken in this Earth dream. You can tap into your star's Akashic records and uncover your non-physical energetic gifts and watch as they show up in the physical. As a collective soul, we can grant ourselves access to the energetic records of all spiritual gifts. Next, we will gift you with techniques to do so.

Grounding Technique to Access Spiritual Gifts

One of the easiest methods to ground is to place the thought of highest source in the forefront of your mind; this will open your third eye completely. Next, imagine light roots growing from the soles of your feet into the ground, wrapping around Gaia 111 times. When you are in this quantum space, ask questions and the energetic answers will be infused through the light roots in your feet up through your body, all the way to the heart of your soul. You can ask, "What is my most organic gift?" Then, become aware of it. You may get an audible response. Witness it as it activates. Just like any muscle, with any spiritual gift, we must use it to make it grow stronger. In future chapters, we will go into detail on how to activate each, individual gift.

It's great to combine and use the technique above while going barefoot and standing in the dirt. Use the same technique and breathe in Source Gaia's green and pink organic light up through the light roots in your feet, into all your chakra systems, clearing and updating them with the most organic light information. Bring this light all the way to the heart of your soul; it's right inside of you. Just believe in it to access it. This connects you to the collective soul, the Source Sun, no matter where you are energetically. From here, you will gain access to your star Akashic records.

You can use this technique to access spiritual gifts or any information you are curious about. The key to opening this doorway is doing it for the greatest good of all in whatever information or gifts you are asking to receive, or your access will be denied to the highest light records.

Questions to ask:

- What is my most blissful gift?

- What gift will give me financial freedom?

- What is my most fun gift?

- What gift will expand the collective consciousness with ease and grace?

- How can I best utilize my gifts?

You may get an audible response, a visual one, or a sign later that day through a variety of ways, such as a post, a song, or from the mouth of a stranger. The answer you seek could come from anywhere, that's how divine energy works. When you get the answer to your question, we want you to acknowledge the gift and witness in your heart through seeing, knowing, or feeling, the gift coming online. This is a process, treat it like any muscle; the more you use it, the more it grows. You are a ray of source; when you ask the questions, the answers will come. Start by asking one question a day and remember the question throughout the day until you get a response.

We, David and Francesca, are at a point now where we can instantly connect to source level, ask any question, and receive a response. However, we, too, had to start slow and practice to become pros. This process works best if you stay focused on one question and answer at a time. Practice your most organic gift daily. This is how we became such strong channels of source energy. We practiced every day and shared all that we received with anyone who would listen.

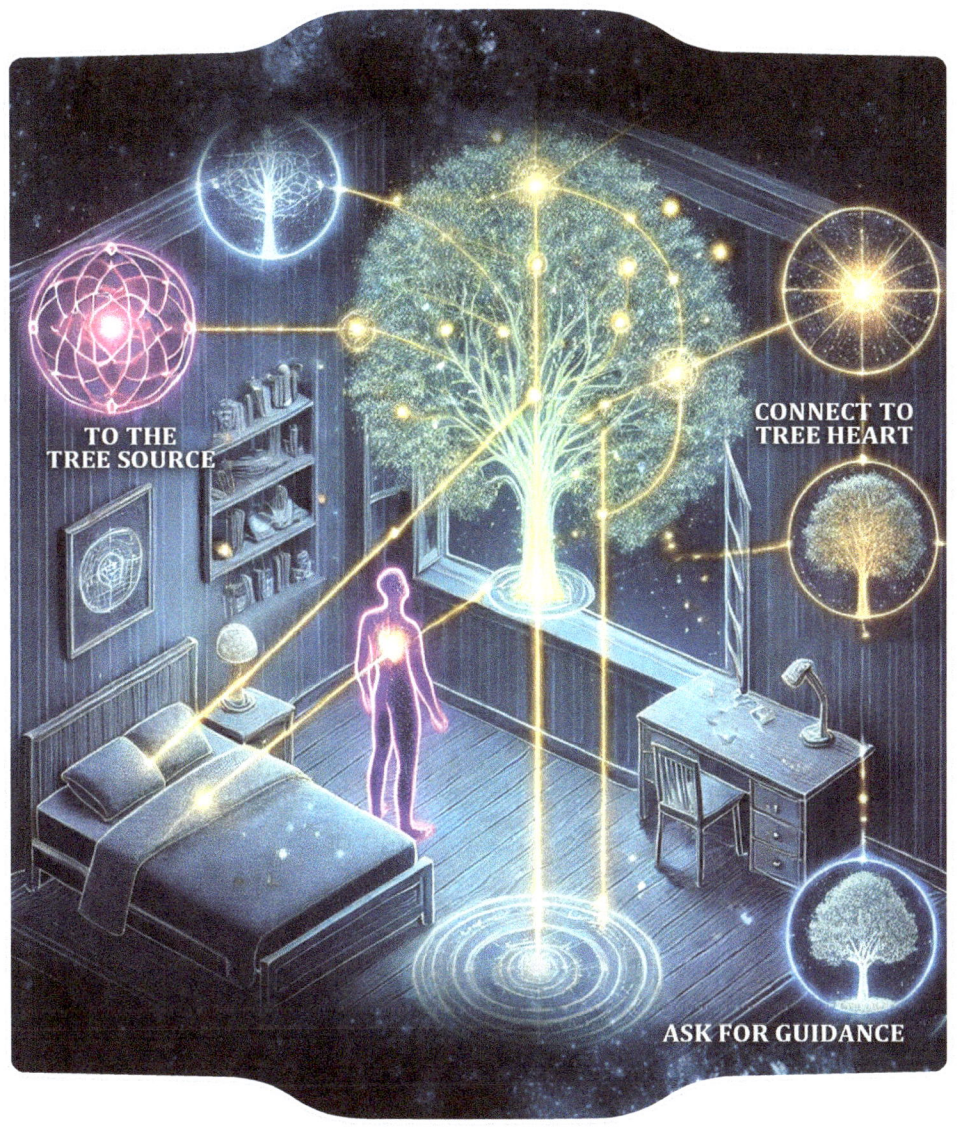

The Tree Collective Grounding Technique

For this technique, project your light and heart energy into the heart energy of a tree. Visualize your energy going down the tree and out through its roots into Gaia. Then, intend to connect to all the trees around you and expand until you are connected to every tree on the planet. This will help you ground. This method is particularly useful in extreme cases, where you may be experiencing major upgrades and have so much light that you need to calm down and become more present in your body.

Many people experience major chakra upgrades, and sometimes they need more than grounding techniques to support them. For example, you may find yourself with excess energy and a racing heart, so we want to share a way for you to return to yourself, out of anxiety, and into relaxation.

As your heart races while expanding into a higher love frequency, you are literally ascending your frequency. When this happens, the key is the breath. Focus on your breath, directing it into your heart with your intentions, and say the word "calm." As you exhale, say the word "calm." Repeat "calm" on the inhale and "calm" on the exhale, over and over again, up to 1000 times if needed, until your heart rate slows. This technique is for when advanced grounding methods are required.

Concurrently, as you inhale, visualize the light going through your chakras. Visualize it leaving your feet, bringing awareness to feeling it integrate into Gaia. As this happens, continue breathing in "calm" and exhaling "calm." Ascending can sometimes put you in these situations, but reaching a higher frequency is worth it, and these techniques will help you through the process.

Water Grounding Technique

When in the shower you can send your light into the water droplets. As the water droplets go down the drain, the light goes into Gaia. Focusing on the water will help you ground and take the excess light off you. The key is to have awareness and intention. The awareness of the sound of the water, the awareness of your light going into those droplets, and the intention for the light to go fluidly from you to the droplets and into the drain, grounding into Gaia. This technique can be such a peaceful experience.

Practicing Grounding Techniques

Now that we have taught you how to ground, we will guide you through a meditation to provide you with high-frequency energy so you can practice your grounding techniques.

Step 1. Call on a golden light angel to come to you.

Step 2. Ask the golden light angel to bring you into the crystalline source energy inside your heart chakra.

Step 3. Breathe into this crystalline source energy and exhale it above, below, and beside your auric field. Repeat this breath at least 20 times while feeling all the crystalline energies.

Step 4. Re-read these grounding techniques and choose your favorite way to ground the light you just manifested.

CHAPTER 5
ACCESSING YOUR AKASHIC RECORDS
Accessing Your Akashic Records

The Star Akashic Records are composed vibrationally and represent the compilation of all Omni-events that have occurred in the past, present, or future, in terms of all energetic forms. These records exist in the non-physical plane of existence and can be accessed from anywhere, utilized in the creation of physical manifestations.

The easiest way to access your Star Records is as follows:

- Clear Your Inner and Outer Space: Prepare for interdimensional travels by ensuring both your inner and outer environments are clear.

- Set Sacred Space: Establish a sacred space, as discussed in the previous chapter.

- Ground: Begin with grounding techniques (reference Chapter 4 for grounding techniques or use your own).

- Open Your Heart: Visualize or set your intention to open the front and back of your heart, preparing to access the records. Then proceed with the following steps:

  » Become a Conscious Explorer: Enter the realm of your heart where the records can be accessed.

  » Call on Omni Source Energy: Invoke the assistance of angels, guides, galactics, elementals, ancestors, or any energy you resonate with to aid in accessing the records. If you're unsure or new to this process, using a guide is beneficial.

» Visualization Technique: For visual learners, visualize your Akashic records as a library. Imagine pulling down a book that contains the information you seek. Witness the information downloading into your hands. If visualization isn't your strength, set the intention to download the information directly.

» Integration and Practice: After downloading information, integrate it into your being. Practice using the new knowledge or gift before returning to the records for more. This approach prevents overwhelming yourself.

Remember, you can access any information from the Akashic Records. The key to utilizing this information for the highest light energy is to intend it to be used for the greatest good of all. If your intentions are not aligned with this principle, you may download information that contains shadows or is not aligned with the highest evolved source light.

Accessing Your Crystalline Akashic Records

There are many belief systems out there regarding how to access your Akashic Records. Akashic Records exist within everyone. Not only in your DNA but also in your heart chakra. The ultimate records exist in your crystalline consciousness, known as the Crystalline Akashic Records. The Crystalline Akashic Records encompass all records, including galactic records, Earth records, and all universal Akashic Records of every lifetime and existence you have ever lived.

Setting Intentions

When accessing your Akashic Records it's essential to set clear and pure intentions. The divine encourages releasing density, embodying light, letting go of old patterns, and embracing self-love and purity. This process can help you learn about your past lives and release negative karma. Whether new to this journey or experienced, starting with intentions aimed at your highest good is crucial. Avoid intentions driven by greed, as this will not lead to true empowerment.

Clearing density is a powerful way to use the Akashic Records. You can clear lifetimes where you experienced or caused emotional, physical, or sexual abuse. By forgiving yourself and others, sending healing to your heart, and calling in angels to fill you with golden light, you can replace the density with a high-vibrational frequency of love. This process ensures there is no void in your energy, promoting healing and balance.

Power retrieval is another significant aspect of working with the Akashic Records. By merging with powerful aspects of your past lives, you can reclaim gifts and abilities that enhance your consciousness and provide a deeper understanding of your existence. Techniques like calling on lifetimes where you mastered your consciousness or where you were a great healer can activate these energies within you now and expand your awareness.

When accessing the records, meditation and visualization are key techniques. Deep meditation helps you enter a state where you can visualize a sacred space or a hall of records. Using specific prayers or invocations, setting protective shields, and employing crystals like clear quartz or selenite can enhance your connection and clarity. Keeping a journal to record your experiences and insights is also beneficial.

Interpreting the messages and symbols you receive is crucial. Pay attention to recurring themes, symbols, and emotional responses, as they often hold significant meaning. Reflecting on this information and integrating it into your daily life can provide practical steps for personal growth.

Ethical considerations are vital, especially when accessing the records for others. Always seek permission, respect confidentiality, and work with the highest intentions. Advanced practices, such as working with ascended masters and exploring higher dimensions within the records, can offer deeper insights and healing opportunities. Through past life healing and soul retrieval, you can address traumas affecting your current life and reclaim lost aspects of your soul.

Soul Fragments and Retrieval

Throughout our lifetimes, particularly during traumatic events, parts of our soul can fragment and become lost or disconnected. This was also discussed in Chapter 3 regarding Inner Child Healing. This process, known as soul fragmentation, often occurs as a protective mechanism to help us cope with severe emotional, physical, or psychological pain. While this can be helpful in the short term, over time these lost fragments can lead to feelings of incompleteness, emotional numbness, or a sense of disconnection from our true selves.

Retrieving these soul fragments is a crucial step towards becoming a whole soul again. By accessing the Akashic Records, you can identify and retrieve these lost pieces. This process involves journeying back to the moments of trauma, acknowledging the pain, and inviting the fragmented parts of your soul to return to you. Using techniques like deep meditation, visualization, and calling upon your higher self and spiritual guides, you can guide these fragments back into your heart, where they can be reintegrated.

As you retrieve and reintegrate these soul fragments, you may experience profound healing and a renewed sense of wholeness. This process helps to heal old wounds, restore your energy, and reconnect you with your true essence. Over time, you will notice increased emotional resilience, a deeper connection to your inner self, and a greater sense of peace and harmony in your life. Through this journey of soul retrieval, you are not only healing the past but also empowering yourself to live more fully in the present as a complete and unified soul.

CHAPTER 6
THE FIRST GIFT ACTIVATION
Channeling

    Channeling is streaming different energy in the form of messages from different energetic sources. There are many ways to channel messages. Here are our ways to help activate this gift that is already inside of you, waiting to be discovered, uncovered, and used.

We, David and Francesca, can channel into any energy because it has always been strong within us. We practiced extensively on social media, spreading unity consciousness, consciousness expansion, and aligning with divinity for peace on Earth and Earth's evolutionary expansion. We both had very similar visions of world peace, which is how we met each other and much of our soul family. For this, we are beyond grateful.

The Heart Portal

The heart portal is the key. Everything, including your guides, your higher self, and Mother Father God, is connected within your heart. The biggest questions everyone has are: How do you find them? What if you can't see them? What if you can't hear them? The first step into channeling is developing a relationship and trust with the heart. Start by asking your heart questions and seeking yes or no answers. Listen for the response with your heart—you will know if it's a yes or no. This develops the foundational relationship and trust with your heart necessary for more advanced channeling.

Resonance and Truth

Channeling takes time to develop, and some may grasp it sooner than others. The key is developing resonance, which is when the heart's frequency knows if the information is correct or not. This is why asking your heart questions is crucial. David recalls, "It took me 17 days to receive my first angelic channeling. I sat in meditation, asking for divine messages. When I heard a voice saying, 'Hi David, this is Archangel Raphael, I have a divine message for you.' I responded by asking for something I didn't know. If the being couldn't provide new information, I would dismiss it as my imagination. On day 17, an angel identified as Archangel Metatron came to me and said, 'Hi David. I am Archangel Metatron.' When I asked for something I didn't know he informed me about the discovery of an 8th color in the rainbow that is invisible and can be seen only through infrared. I immediately googled this information and found that NASA had recently discovered an invisible 8th color in the rainbow through bomb detonation. Although I didn't fully understand the connection between bomb detonation and infrared, this experience was both specific and special to me. I continued channeling Archangel Metatron for almost a year, which led me to realize that everything is consciousness. I progressed to channeling trees and ascended masters, and through the process, received profound wisdom."

Francesca started channeling messages as a small child but did not realize it was a gift. We all can channel if we listen and question the little voices inside our minds. The more you acknowledge the messages, the more frequently you will receive energetic visitations from non-physical energy within your soul system or inner solar system.

Francesca says, "Since I was 3, many would say I had no filter and that I was a chatterbox because the most random things would always fly out of my mouth. I would always shock myself. I often had different angelic voices communicating with me and I would listen and say whatever I heard. There was no thinking involved. I remember when I was 4, my mother lost a very expensive diamond and my guardian angel told me the exact location of the diamond. I knew then I had some nice friends I could not see but could hear and feel. As I got older, I could see many other worldly things within my mind's eye, allowing me to put faces to the voices I channeled.

The gift of channeling affords me the opportunity to know what to say to help people feel better because I can receive messages of hope and enlightenment from other's guardian angels, guides, and source selves. People throughout my whole life have come to me for comfort and guidance, and it has been an honor to serve the divine in this way. In visions, I saw that I am a spirit guide myself, and in this life, beings that I guided in the past are now guiding me. This is my first lifetime on this Earth, so I have been shown that I have been an Omni-guide my whole existence, and now it's my turn to experience human life.

It's a great blessing I am so ancient and such an open channel that I can allow everything and everyone in their source energy to stream messages through me. I have impeccable discernment. As long as the transmissions are loving I know it is of divine origin. Any messages that are not of love, I question and dissect until I get to the root of what's being communicated to me. If a message is negative, I provide it with the justice it deserves and listen to it until we shed light onto the true layer of love it has hidden inside. All energy, physical or non-physical, wants to be acknowledged and loved.

Embracing my channeling gift has made my life very entertaining because I am never alone and always have messages pouring in. I know virtually every being from my ethereal career as an Omni-guide, so I can basically channel anyone and anything as we are all one big holy family, and I have established open contact within myself."

High-level channeling outside yourself requires proper training. Introducing the concept of working with light removes the need for conscious thought—you simply trust that the light knows. One of our biggest secrets is working with golden light angels, as they are among the highest vibrational angels. Their motto is: "How can I assist and love more?" They will always guide you to where you need to be as long as it is within the love frequency.

Connecting with Golden Light Angels

As mentioned in Chapter 2, it is crucial to connect your pillar of light because the golden light angels travel down the pillars of light. After connecting your pillar of light, call on a golden light angel to descend it. Trust they will be present. Ask them to guide you into your heart and upward to your higher self because you have a question. Visualize or feel yourself flying into your heart with their guidance. You will know when you reach your higher self because the golden light angel will guide you there—just trust.

Tree Channeling

Tree channeling is an easy and wonderful introduction to channeling. Go outside, find a tree, and place your hand on it. Breathe into your heart and exhale your heart energy into the tree, connecting with the tree's heart energy. In this beautiful connection, ask the tree, "What do I need to know the most right now?" Listen with your heart—it's truly a magical experience. The heart-to-heart frequency connection is the key to channeling, and it's essential to utilize this when trusting what you channel. You can always trust a tree. You can always trust your heart.

However, channeling beyond this without proper discernment of the light isn't advisable due to the existing polarity within this reality. You want to avoid channeling lower vibrational energy. To discern light energy from lower vibrational trickster energy, one must acknowledge the feelings of the energy as it streams in. If it feels good and loving, it is the light. If it gives you fear or uneasy feelings, you must cast it into the light of source.

Activating Your Channeling Gift

When you are new to channeling, one of the best ways to activate your channeling gift is to get a pen and paper (a computer also works). After you clear yourself, set sacred space, and ground, set an intention. This helps ensure you channel the highest source light beings instead of trickster energies, like demonic energy.

The first thing we recommend is asking a question like, "What being of pure source light would like to channel through me?" and start writing. Write anything that comes to mind. Do this for a week straight and watch as the floodgates of information pour in. Ask whatever questions you are curious about. For example, you could ask for the name of your guardian angel. Once you know the name of the beings you are channeling, it re-establishes your connection and puts you into contact with them. You can call on that energy, or you can call on new energies to come in and ask them questions. Think of yourself as a divine reporter getting to know the energies that exist inside of you, as we house all inside and have access to unlimited worlds of information. Don't get discouraged if you get weird messages that don't make sense at first. It will all come together the more you practice.

When you begin to channel, to avoid fearful energies streaming through, start with the highest heaven and angels because their energy is sweet and pure. If it feels good, continue with the channeling. If it feels bad, ask the energy to leave three times. It's energetic law, it must leave. Until you become proficient at channeling, it is best to cast negative energy into the light of Source with intention. When you become advanced in channeling and want to explore negative energies, it can lead to shadow work and uncovering more light. Wait to explore negative energies until you are completely comfortable discerning the energy and how it makes you feel using questions. If an energy feels negative, ask three times, "Is this the highest source energy?" and it must answer honestly. If it says "No," respond three times, "You must leave," with the intention that it goes back to pure source light to be purified and recycled into a higher love energy. The beings that come through that are not of the highest source light appreciate this because they want to be loved, and this gets them to their most favorable state of beingness.

Expanding Your Channeling Experience

Continue the channeling process with questions. Start by asking your guardian angel to channel through you. You are always safe to ask your heart to send a guide that resonates highly with you, like fairies, to message through you. Our hearts will never steer us wrong, so using your heart as a guidance tool is always beneficial.

Once you become proficient at channeling, you will easily be able to call in your highest guides for anything. If you want a new gift, for example, you can call in the highest light master of spiritual gifts to activate you. It's often a fun surprise when you first start. You never know who might show up to party with you. Honestly, using your imagination is key in the channeling process because you are unlimited in what energies you can bring into your awareness. Each energy you channel will bring different gifts, activations, feelings, emotions, voices, angles, perspectives, and points of view.

Amplifying Your Channeling Gifts

Other things we did to amplify our channeling gifts included giving private readings, where messages would come through to help others. We gained our unlimited access keys to channeling by wanting to help everyone for the greatest good of all. Channeling is second nature to us, and it keeps expanding. If you practice, it will grow quickly within you.

Other great ways to enhance your channeling gifts are to surround yourself with the energies you desire to channel. For example, if you want to channel fairies, open your heart and call them in. It helps to set the mood in a way that invokes the feelings of the energy you are trying to conjure within you. To channel fairies, go out in nature, especially around gardens, because fairies love flowers. Wear crystals because fairies love sparkle. Customize your channeling experience to feel like the energy you wish to channel. If you want to channel an ascended master, take up yoga or tai chi. If you want to channel a movie star, watch a documentary about them and wear an outfit they would wear. If you want to channel mermaids, read about Atlantis, go to the beach, and surround yourself with seashells. It's all about getting into the mindset of that energy. There is no wrong way to get into the mood. As long as the scene you are setting puts you in the thought and feeling of the energy, you will align with the wavelength the specific energy exists in.

You can also buy oracle decks with whatever theme you are channeling. Oracle decks are filled with energetic codes. Read stories about angels and get into the mindset of the angelics if you want to connect to their wavelength. We, David and Francesca, are at the level now where we know these energies exist within our hearts. We just tap in through our hearts with intention and go through our source stream channel directly to the energies. But that is after practicing this gift for a very long time. We are at the point where we have energies ask us to channel them, and messages pour in non-stop throughout the day from a multitude of different energetic streams of consciousness. What you seek is seeking you, and the gift of channeling has already been trying to communicate with you if you are interested in it. Listen to the voices in your head;

ask them what they are trying to communicate to you and use your discernment to engage with them or cast them into the light of source. It's much easier than you think and innate in us all.

Exercise to Activate Your Channeling Gift

1. Prepare Your Space: Find a quiet and comfortable place where you won't be disturbed. Create sacred space by lighting a candle, burning incense, or playing soft, calming music. Ensure you have a journal and a pen nearby.

2. Ground Yourself: Sit or lie down in a relaxed position. Close your eyes and take several deep breaths. Visualize roots extending from your feet or base of your spine into the earth, grounding you and connecting you with the Earth's energy.

3. Center Your Mind: Focus on your breathing, letting go of any thoughts or distractions. Imagine a warm, golden light entering through the top of your head, filling your entire being with peace and tranquility.

4. Open Your Heart Chakra: Place your hand over your heart and visualize a radiant pink light glowing from your heart chakra. See this light expanding and enveloping you in its warmth and love. Feel the connection to the divine and to your higher self.

5. Set Your Intention: Silently or out loud, set the intention to connect with your higher self, spirit guides, or any benevolent beings who wish to communicate with you. Invite them to come forward and share their wisdom.

6. Listen and Receive: Sit quietly with your eyes closed, staying

open to any impressions, words, or images that come to you. Trust whatever you receive, even if it feels subtle or uncertain.

7. Write and Reflect: Open your journal and begin to write down any messages, feelings, or insights you received during the exercise. Don't judge or filter your words—let them flow freely.

8. Express Gratitude: Thank your higher self, spirit guides, or any beings who communicated with you. Express gratitude for their guidance and love.

9. Close the Session: Visualize the pink light from your heart chakra gently retracting back into your heart. Take a few more deep breaths, and when you're ready, open your eyes.

10. Practice Regularly: Make this exercise a regular part of your spiritual practice to strengthen your connection and enhance your channeling abilities.

CHAPTER 7
THE SECOND GIFT ACTIVATION
DIMENSIONAL JUMPING

A Warning in Dimensional Jumping

There are some fundamentals to dimensional jumping that everyone needs to know. First, you need to anchor. What is anchoring? Anchoring is tethering your light into the heart of Gaia (Earth). Why is it important? Because if you jump or astral travel to dimensions without anchoring, you can disconnect permanently from your body. It's a serious warning and not something to play with. Another risk is that you may untether and enter another dimension, leaving a part of yourself behind. This can lead to a psychotic episode because your body remains on Earth while your energy is elsewhere. Respect your energy and always ground before dimensional jumping.

IF THIS HAPPENS: Call back your light by saying, "I call back my light from all realities, timelines, and dimensions to be with me now." Then, feel yourself come back.

Many people over the years have gone on astral journeys and come back with a headache or feeling that there are entities around them. The reason this occurs is that they traveled outside of themselves and left a piece of their consciousness in another false dimensional construct, where they may have picked up an etheric energy that is not of the light. David and Francesca have traveled extensively in all dimensions and want you to be aware: **YOU HAVE ALL YOU NEED WITHIN**. Do not travel outside of yourself unless it is to go inside the eye of the sun. You can reach any planet, any celestial system by going through the Universe of Self in your heart portal. It's the safest way to travel, as you won't pick up any etheric attachments. Furthermore, you can never get lost inside yourself.

It is important to understand that all dimensions, all consciousness, and everything exists inside of you. You are literally a walking omniverse, a God-creator being. It's important to know there are other God-creators and energetic beings creating from different streams of consciousness, so you can easily get crossed with the wrong energy during astral travel.

David will never forget the day Christ came to him to teach him the lessons of going within the heart. He told David he would be training him. Christ started working with David on heart awareness and helped him realize everything is within. That changed David's life, and from that day, David has always gone through the heart portal, except when sungazing, because the origin source is within the sun and everything inside the sun is pure love.

Another key rule is to have an intention. Where are you going? Intention sets up the energy to follow. Without intention, you could end up anywhere. One of David's first out-of-body experiences occurred without intention. He ended up in a very high-energy dimension and brought back a strange vibrating energy with him. The effect of this energy was bothersome to his family for over a year until he finally cleared it out.

Francesca's first out-of-body experience landed her in a hell dimension where she had to communicate with and clear lower vibrational energies because she did not set an intention. Luckily, she remembered to call on all the angels in heaven to assist her, which they did. Though

she came back stronger, she was very scared. These unpleasant experiences could have been avoided with clear intentions.

So, where do you want to go? The key lies in understanding that you can go anywhere. The universe is infinite, and consciousness will take you where you intend.

Levels of Consciousness

It's helpful to understand the levels of consciousness. The higher the level you access, the higher the frequency you embody. For example, **Crystalline Consciousness** is above carbon-based reality. In this dimension, you experience very high energy, can program crystals, connect with crystal aspects, and access your crystalline Akashic Records for universal or Earth past lives.

The Diamond Dimension is even higher than the crystalline and holds some of the purest levels of consciousness within our universal structure. Many past lives, including those of Yeshua Christ, are connected within the Diamond level, supporting physical reality with purity and love frequency. Additionally, you can connect with **Universal Consciousness,** tapping into galactic aspects such as the Arcturians, Sirians, Pleiadians, Andromedans, and Lyrans. These universal galactic beings are dedicated to universal peace and assisting species throughout the universe in their evolution.

Humans are destined to join Universal Consciousness collectively and become peacekeepers within the galaxy, joining galactic fleets to assist all life forms in their evolution.

Beyond this, there are God Consciousness and Master Consciousness levels, which empower your Christ consciousness and innate supernatural gifts. Above these is Alpha Omega, the creation of prime source energetic beings who create universes, planets, star systems, and consciousness at all levels of creation. They hold all the origin templates and eternity codes.

Exploring these levels of consciousness and dimensions takes time, but with the assistance of golden light angels and clear intentions to find these levels within your heart chakra, your adventures will begin.

Dimensional jumping is an inside game and the beginning of your interdimensional travels. You must have a deep wish to know the source within yourself and be willing to heal, remove all false conditioning, and peel away all your false belief systems to tap into different dimensions. The great part is that we have all the dimensions inside ourselves; this is an energetic journey we can all embark on to explore lands never heard of before. This is how many movies and books were created—in dimensions within ourselves that do exist, just not on the Earth plane currently, unless we decide as a collective to harness them.

Starting with Guided Meditations

One way to start the dimensional jumping process is by beginning with guided meditations to prime you or start meditating for a couple of minutes a day—just close your eyes without sleeping and see what pops into your head. Both ways are effective depending on your goal. When you use others' guided meditations, you will jump into the dimensions they have already explored. You can expand and keep going in that dimension, or if you meditate on your own, you can go to new lands within yourself that have not been explored. The key is to do this as much as you can. For us, life is a walking meditation where we are constantly going in and out of dimensions inside ourselves. We could be walking our dogs, connecting our hearts to a tree, and our energy will jump into Middle Earth or any random dimension where we download messages and codes.

Once you become good at meditating, the more you practice wakeful meditations while doing other tasks, the more you will jump into dimensions all the time without trying. As humans, we often naturally jump into different dimensions and realms; we are just not aware of it. Each time we make a positive choice, we expand into a higher dimensional energy. For example, a thought of the fairy realm might pop into your head, and before you know it, visions and messages pour in while a dragonfly flies by as an archetypal reflection of your inner reality.

When you heal from traumas, you will uncover more of your light and gain access to higher realms, such as the dimension of highest heaven. You have to raise your vibration really high to get there and stay there. When you feel in love, you are in the highest heaven; you are just not aware you are in that dimension of yourself. When you feel bad and disconnected from everyone else, you are in a lower dimension, which is why many depressed people turn to drugs—they get stuck in lower dimensions within themselves and use substances to disconnect from their current reality.

We all have free will and can always call on guides and angels to assist us; their non-physical energy will pull you out of the lower dimensional realms. All of our higher energetic aspects are waiting to assist us from every dimension of self. They are awaiting our call. When we started our journey, we had to clear energies from past lives and for the collective energy, which sometimes pulled us down to the lower realms. We developed energetic safety practices to help us rise when we descended into lower dimensional realities.

The most important thing to remember, wherever you are, is to call on your source light and witness this connection that never left you. This will clear your pains and heal your heart by forgiving others and yourself, allowing you to be in higher dimensional states that require you to raise your vibration. We love to be in higher dimensional states of consciousness where the reality of the fun dimensions exists—there are endless ones. A few of the fun dimensions we really enjoy are the magic, galactic, fairy, God, and

Goddess realms. You must do the spiritual healing work of raising your vibration to access the keys to the most beautiful dimensional doorways.

Don't forget to ground yourself; it's always the first step. As enjoyable as it is to explore these levels of consciousness, it's crucial to remain grounded so you can appreciate life on Earth. After all, we are human and here to enjoy this beautiful planet. When you ground, you integrate these energies from the higher realms and fully activate their high vibrational codes within you.

Joy Dimensional Jumping: A Step-by-Step Guide to Enter Joy Consciousness in the Heart

1. *Set Sacred Space:*

- Find a quiet and comfortable place where you won't be disturbed.

- Light a candle and place it in front of you to signify the sacred space.

- Optionally, burn incense or diffuse essential oils such as lavender or rose to create a calming atmosphere.

- Arrange crystals or sacred objects around you to enhance the sacredness of the space.

2. *Ground Yourself:*

- Sit or lie down in a relaxed position.

- Close your eyes and take several deep breaths.

- Visualize roots extending from your feet or base of your spine deep into the Earth, anchoring you to the Earth's energy.

3. *Center Your Mind:*

- Focus on your breathing, letting go of any thoughts or distractions.

- Imagine a warm, golden light entering through the top of your head, filling your entire being with peace and tranquility.

4. *Call Upon the Golden Light Angel:*

- Silently or aloud, invite a Golden Light Angel to assist you in this journey.

- Visualize this angel appearing before you, radiating golden light and warmth.

- Feel the angel's presence surrounding you with love and protection.

5. *Open Your Heart Chakra: Open Your Heart Chakra:*

- Place your hand over your heart and visualize a radiant pink light glowing from your heart chakra.

- See this light expanding and enveloping you in its warmth and love.

- Feel the connection to the divine and to your higher self.

6. *Invoke Joy Consciousness:*

- Ask the Golden Light Angel to guide you into the joy consciousness within your heart.

- Visualize the angel touching your heart chakra with a golden light, activating the joy consciousness within.

- Feel waves of joy and happiness spreading throughout your heart and entire being.

7. *Breathe in Joy Consciousness Energies:*

- Take deep, slow breaths, inhaling the golden light of joy consciousness.

- With each breath, feel the joy consciousness energies filling your auric field, radiating outward from your heart.

- Visualize your aura glowing with vibrant, golden light, filled with joy and happiness.

8. *Embrace the Joy Consciousness:*

- Allow yourself to fully experience the joy consciousness within your heart.

- Feel the joy permeating every cell of your body, mind, and spirit.

- Stay in this state of joy for as long as you feel comfortable.

9. Express Gratitude:

- Thank the Golden Light Angel for guiding you into the joy consciousness.

- Express gratitude for the experience and the joy you received.

10. Close the Session:

- Visualize the golden light gently retracting back into your heart.

- Take a few more deep breaths, grounding yourself back into the present moment.

- When you're ready, open your eyes and take a moment to reflect on the experience.

11. Practice Regularly:

- Make Joy Dimensional Jumping a regular part of your spiritual practice to strengthen your connection to joy consciousness and maintain a high vibrational state.

CHAPTER 8
THE THIRD GIFT ACTIVATION
Guides

Welcome to the journey of the Omni-dimensional being. Before sharing how to activate guides, we will explain why it's important to activate guides. Guides can see most of your timelines and connect you to your higher timelines. They provide the guidance and direction you need in life. Similar to Cupid shooting arrows that connect you to where you need to go. Ultimately, you are meant to be your own master, but there are many benefits to connecting with guides.

In addition to life direction, guides offer frequency integration. When you merge with guides, you can come into higher frequencies, as long as you merge with guides of light. This is why it's important to be intentional when you call in guides. There are many types of guides: your angel guides who assist with your life path, galactic guides who assist with higher knowledge and frequency, ascended masters who assist you with your master templates and Christed light, and even fairy guides, elemental guides, and family, who have passed—you name it, you can tap into it. It's important to know why you need a guide.

Most people want guides for abundance or love, but they miss the true meaning of abundance, which is being in joy and self-love in all that you are. It's not that financial abundance isn't important because we all have to survive, but the guides of light want to assist you to rise above this. They want you to become your own master and begin creating and manifesting as the god consciousness you are. Until you reach these levels, it's easy to activate your guides.

The heart portal—all the guides are here: the higher self, the galactic guides, and all the realms of light. It's the safest way to travel and connect. It's the universe within and it mirrors the universe without or outside of you. As above, so below; all is ONE. Accessing your guides can be as easy as calling in a golden light angel and asking them to bring you into your universal consciousness within your heart or your angelic consciousness within your heart. Are you ready to meet your angelic self? I have an ANGEL SELF? Yes, everyone does, and you can connect with this beautiful magical winged being of light through the angelic consciousness.

Many have already established relationships with deities, whether they are masters like Buddha, Krishna, or Yeshua. It is as easy as intending to build up the heart frequency to connect with their heart frequency. You call them in, focus on the frequency of their heart, connecting it to the frequency of your heart, until they arrive, and you can feel them. Some need protection, some need divine light, and calling them in while building heart frequency is the way to truly bring them in.

Our guides want us to reach out. You can start activating your guides today by calling on the highest source light to please send you a guide to assist you. You have to be clear on what type of guide you want to assist you and discern when they come in if they are the right guide for you. If they don't feel like love, they are not source guides—they are a lower energetic projection comprised of your wounding, plain and simple.

We have so many guides within us. It's a matter of choosing the right ones. Guides can change as you want them to or as you change, vibrating differently during the different chapters of your life. The first thing you need to know about guides is they are you at different frequencies and different dimensions, assisting you from whatever world, realm, planet, and dimension they are in. It's different energetic versions of you waiting on your call to assist you, and you can even merge these aspects with you if you resonate highly with their energy.

The first step is to put out the call. Be clear in your mind what type of guide you want and what you need the guide for. Be open, and don't be scared. Fear is an energetic obstacle that will block you from your guide. So, you must get into the right mental mind state to be clear of blockages that will hinder your guides from connecting.

When the guides come in, be open to their messages, but remember you are the one driving the ship. You can say no, choosing to do things your own way as this is your life experience. Always discern their guidance and do the things that feel good to your heart. In our experience, guides will sometimes support you through lessons that you must learn the hard way. They could jump you through the experience, but that would allow you to spiritually bypass the situation, hindering you from learning the full lesson. Sometimes we need to taste the bitter to appreciate the sweet.

Humanity is moving toward a time of the end of suffering. Guides and energies are becoming more accessible from the dimensions of the highest vibrational source energy. This kind of open, source contact occurring in our human evolution provides messages to help us end suffering and remain in our bliss. As such, it has been in our best interest to listen to our guides. When we do not listen to divine advice, we suffer a little bit. There are consequences to not listening to the highest light advice. This is why you need to be on your high vibrational game and think about what you do want because it will show up in your reality.

We highly recommend reading Rhonda Byrne's The Secret and Abraham Hicks' The Vortex if you struggle with negativity. These books are the bibles of raising your vibration and are worth the investment for their energetic codes alone.

You can keep guides for life. They will have a special way of communicating with you. We, David and Francesca, just think of our guides and their energy shows up. Sometimes new guides will emerge naturally when you are open to receiving assistance with a grateful and open heart. Always thank the guides. Guides will become your best friends. Additionally, it becomes easier to detach from negative people and energies around you when you have non-physical beings assisting you.

Another method to connect with a guide is to open the front and back of your heart, walk through to your Akashic Records, and call on a guide of the highest source light to assist you. Your Akashic Records are within your heart portal, and the quickest way to access them is to ask for a specific guide or a guide for your highest good to stream their energy through you. It's important to understand that every record of every life and experience is stored within you as a vibration. When you ask for the light stream to come in, it connects to that vibrational storage area within the heart.

You can access your records for various reasons, such as retrieving higher consciousness frequencies from past experiences, which activates your DNA and expands your light frequency. You might also access the records to release negative vibrations that keep you in a similar karmic loop or pattern in your life. For example, if you are often betrayed, you can call on the root lifetime of your first betrayal to heal that wound. You can also access records simply to see experiences, such as a perfect lifetime.

Dense vibrations within may appear as black cords that lead to a lifetime where a negative experience occurred and needs healing. Higher consciousness and sacred lifetimes appear as gold cords that lead to moments when you embodied your divine, higher consciousness. The concept is to follow the strand of light to a particular lifetime and bring awareness to what is happening in that moment. A straightforward way to find yourself in a lifetime is to scan your energy field in the present moment and match it to your energy field in the lifetime you are exploring. Then, bring awareness to the environment: where you are, who is there, and what is happening. This will give you the perspective needed to fulfill the divine purpose of why you are being guided to this lifetime, all for your highest good.

When you perform healing work on lifetimes, especially when dealing with trauma or negative experiences, you not only break the energetic loop pattern in your current life but also raise your vibration and expand your consciousness. The entire purpose of this work is to come into your power and divine self.

When you are ready to access your records and call on your Akashic Record Keepers, ask for your higher self, an angel, or a divine being that is a master energy to come down so the purity levels of free consciousness can shine light on the records you wish to access. This being will then descend from a higher frequency to assist you with whatever you want to explore and access. Angelic guides are the easiest and quickest to respond when called upon. Manifesting guides in your life is all about vibrational alignment.

It is always advisable to create sacred space before starting this work. Call upon an angel or the angelic guard (circle of archangels) for protection. If you wish, you can ask for a name. Once you know the angel's sacred name, you can call upon it at any time, and the energy will appear to assist you.

It is also important to understand chakras and their vertical relationship with your heart's Akashic Records, as the heart does hold all there is. Typically, the third eye records lifetimes of gifts.

You can access these gift lifetimes to discover your abilities or find lifetimes where you blocked your gifts, allowing you to release those blocks.

The throat chakra holds records of lifetimes when you were in your most authentic energy and voice. Here, you can access lifetimes where you excelled in your divine being. What were you doing? These lifetimes are likely similar to the gifts and strengths you have in this lifetime, but they can offer new perspectives and expand your experiences in the present, based on how you excelled as your divine self in the past. Additionally, you can access lifetimes where others blocked your voice or authenticity and clear these blocks so you can shine as your authentic self.

The higher heart chakra, just below your throat chakra, is a gateway to your sacred timelines and your purest light. It is also the key to accessing the highest dimensions of purity that exist. The heart chakra, as you know, is the foundation for all Akashic Records.

The solar plexus chakra contains your power temples. It is excellent for divine connection, power retrieval, and accessing solar temples. This chakra serves as a power center, energizing all chakras and enhancing your divine connection.

The sacral chakra stores your identities and belief systems, including how you feel about yourself, emotional traumas, and reflections of your states of consciousness. You can use this chakra to clear negative beliefs and insecurities in the reflections of your consciousness and access your highest truth and divine source-self beliefs.

The root chakra holds all your relationships—friends, family, lovers, and all relationship experiences, including wonderful and traumatic experiences. Here, you can release all karmic loops related to relationships, allowing you to purify your relationships with yourself and others, avoiding trauma-bonding dynamics.

All of this work assists you in coming into your divine self and raising your frequency. However, there are also other ways to elevate your frequency and attract more love.

Integrating Aspects

If you need more fun in your life, call upon your fairy aspect to embody you. To summon a playful fairy guide, connect your heart with mushrooms, dragonflies, or flowers. This infuses your energetic field with magical fairy codes and magnetizes a fairy guide to you. To receive fairy energy, you must connect with the fairy energetic structures, such as flowers, mushrooms, and dragonflies, which have been seeded here for us. When you infuse enough natural fairy energy to match the fairy codes within you, your fairy guide will appear.

Additionally, you can connect to the fairy grid systems that exist within yourself by breathing into your heart and setting the intention for this connection. As you exhale, activate the fairy grids in your energy field, which will also attract fairy guides.

Galactic guides are much harder to activate within yourself because you must vibrate at a frequency higher than this universal structure to connect with them. This requires detoxifying and purifying your vessel for an extended period. You should also connect your heart to the sun, moon, stars, and planets repeatedly, as long as it takes to make contact with the galactic aspects within yourself. Remember, all are connected, all are ONE, and within you exists all.

To vibrate at a galactic frequency, breathe into your heart and intend to connect to the galactic core energy within you. As you exhale, set the intention to connect with your highest vibrational galactic self, and this guide will come through.

If you want to connect with the Pleiadians, understand that they are both within and without. To connect with them within, breathe into your galactic core, then breathe out and connect with the Pleiadian aspect of yourself that exists alongside you for a divine message. Focus on the heart-to-heart connection of your galactic inner reach and expand it into your field.

You can connect with them externally in many ways, including reading about them on the internet, connecting your heart to theirs when looking at the Pleiadian constellation in the night sky, or engaging with a book about the Pleiadians. You can also receive an energetic exchange with a person who specializes in contact with a particular galactic group, often in an energetic cash exchange for a galactic activation.

If you are not purified and vibrating at a high frequency, this can still activate the energetic codes within you but be prepared to purge all that is of a lower vibration than the galactic energy stream you have tapped into. You will need time to ground, integrate, and anchor the updated energy within yourself. It is advisable to give yourself three days to integrate the new energy.

The energy of the Divine Ones, like Mother Father God, is also easy to connect with. We easily connect with Mother Father God energy because we call them in and keep them at the forefront of our minds. The more we include Mother Father God energy in everything we do, the more guidance from their energy streams through our vessels. Calling on Mother Father God or angels is crucial; they exist to assist but honor free will. If you need angelic assistance, it's like a love hotline to heaven from your intention to connect with them. When they merge their light with yours, it activates your higher Mother Father God energies or your angelic frequencies. You can also find them within yourself, channel them, connect with them, and receive their internal light guidance, all accessed through heart awareness.

Repeatedly focusing your energy on the type of guides you want will harness the activation you need through magnetism, attracting the particular energy you align with. Guides are different versions of you on various energetic wavelengths, so you need to attune yourself to their level. Meditating with the intention of inviting a guide is a beautiful way for random guides to activate within you.

Francesca recounts, "Recently, when I visited Mount Shasta, three Lemurian guides came to bless me and all the spiritual people chanting on the mountain. I saw them flying overhead—each one was blue, and I could see and feel them radiating their beautiful inner Earth mountain energy upon us all. Chanting is a wonderful way to clear yourself and call upon the guides that resonate with musical notes and tones. Guides are unlimited and exist everywhere, both within and without."

Some well-known guides that are fun to connect with are ascended master guides like Quan Yin, Yeshua, and Buddha. You might also connect with galactic guides such as the Lemurians, Venusians, Arcturians, Andromedans, and Lyrans. The magical realms of Earth feature dragons, unicorns, goddesses of air, earth, solar, and water, the Fairy Godmother Collective, the Emerald Order, the Councils of Divinity, the Eternities (light being governance), solar guides, the inner Earth kingdoms, and the sky kingdoms. There are guides and teams of light for every possibility, waiting to connect with you.

However, the most important connection is with yourself. Connect within your heart, stand in your power, and channel your truth from your angelic teams, from Mother Father God within, and from your heart, which holds the eternity of all that is. The purpose of guides is to assist you until you can do it all yourself, but they are also there for you when you need them and when they need you. All assisting all to become the highest divine being, in awareness that you are already this, and letting go of all other beliefs so you can live a life of mastery in full compassion and love for all things, including yourself.

Activating Your Angelic Guides

1. Create a Sacred Space:

    • Find a quiet, comfortable place where you won't be disturbed.

    • Light a candle, burn incense, or play soft, calming music to set the atmosphere.

    • Arrange any sacred objects, crystals, or items that enhance the sacredness of the space.

2. Ground Yourself:

    • Sit or lie down in a relaxed position.

    • Close your eyes and take several deep breaths.

    • Visualize roots extending from your feet or base of your spine deep into the Earth, anchoring you to the Earth's energy.

3. Call Upon a Golden Light Angel:

    • Silently or aloud, invite a Golden Light Angel to assist you in this journey.

    • Visualize this angel appearing before you, radiating golden light and warmth.

    • Feel the angel's presence surrounding you with love and protection.

4. Connect to Your Angelic Source:

- Ask the Golden Light Angel to guide you to the angelic source within your heart.

- Visualize the angel touching your heart chakra with a golden light, activating the angelic source within.

- Feel the divine connection growing stronger with each breath.

5. Breathe in Angelic Light:

- Take a deep breath, inhaling the golden light of the angel into your heart.

- As you exhale, connect with the heart energy of your angelic guides.

- Continue this breathing pattern, feeling the connection deepen with each breath.

6. Ask for a Message:

- In this state of divine connection, silently ask your angelic guides for a message or guidance.

- Remain open and receptive, trusting whatever impressions, words, or feelings come to you.

7. Express Gratitude:

- Thank the Golden Light Angel and your angelic guides for their presence and guidance.

- Feel gratitude for the connection and the messages received.

8. Close the Session:

- Visualize the golden light gently retracting back into your heart.

- Take a few more deep breaths, grounding yourself back into the present moment.

- When you're ready, open your eyes and take a moment to reflect on the experience.

CHAPTER 9
THE FOURTH GIFT ACTIVATION
Healing

Believing you can heal yourself is the first step to healing. Most people rely completely on the medical system, which is largely failing the population. Although there are benefits to surgery and emergency operations, the medical system often prescribes, through big pharma, a dependency on medication that prevents the body from healing itself. However, there are many other ways to calm the mind and heal the body.

Francesca is living proof you can heal yourself, even when doctors and MRIs say you can't. Ten years ago, Francesca was told by doctors that she would not walk again without surgery, following a back injury at work that left her unable to bear weight on her legs due to two severely herniated discs. She used quantum healing methods along with rest, meditation, source healing, positive thought, and faith in the body's self-healing mechanism to heal herself, and now she has no back issues.

As discussed earlier in Chapter 4, shadow work and letting go of density can relieve a lot of sickness and disease as the density energy within you causes most of the sickness. Therefore, it is so important to do your healing work. Your heart is a portal directly connected to your source self. Your heart will remain blocked by your unhealed wounds and that will magnetize broken mirrors to you. Everything does come down to belief, and then belief turns into knowing, and then knowing turns into mastery of healing yourself and others. This is why we must start with belief, but how can you believe if you can't feel? If you can feel the healing, then you know there is healing happening, and that is why we are going to explain how to feel it.

We will give an example that has assisted the toughest clients in feeling. Call on a golden light angel to take you into the angelic consciousness of self in your heart. Trust the golden light angel will bring you to meet your angelic aspect inside your heart in the angelic source light. Once here, intend to connect your heart energy with the heart energy of your angelic self. Breathe in, connecting to your heart energy, and breathe out, connecting to your angelic self's heart energy. You are then going to set the intention on your next breath to connect your heart energy and your angelic self's heart energy. On the exhale, you will blast healing into every cell in your body that needs it. Repeat this for 5 minutes. Connect the angelic healing to your cells and feel the diamond light going into your cells, purifying, healing, and releasing toxicity out of the cells and nervous system. Feel all the toxins leave as the angelic light heals you.

We, as Omni Source Light Creator Beings, all have the ability to heal ourselves. The quickest way to heal is through mind, body, and soul synergetic flow inside of pure Source energy that animates all.

Healing is completed through the God/Source pure vibration. Vibration travels through an electromagnetic wave that is invisible to the human eye, but the magnetic force of healing and creational energy can be felt by all. We are not scientists, but we are evolved humans and can feel our divinity and see it in many ways. We are all Omni Source Light Creator Beings. Those who do not have their seeing gifts (clairvoyance) turned on are not yet able to see it as the seers do.

As your senses begin to evolve, new ones will come online, as it is for us seers, and you will be able to see, sense, and feel with your human senses Source healing energy as it flows through you into another. You will become a witness to the Source energy flowing through all. Seers can see it in many dimensions, another attribute of having your seer abilities coming online.

There is a vibration to everything, and the quickest way to heal is being tapped into and streaming Source-level energy through you, and witnessing your Source oneness, creating a healing current in which miracle energies are birthed.

Healing medicine can be administered through many talents and modalities powered by Source love, such as touch, words, art, song, fashion, architecture, and quantum healing methods, to name a few. Also, connecting with nature or anything that feels good to you can facilitate and amplify your healing abilities.

One of the keys to healing is to be around the people, places, and things, such as pets, that feel loving to you. Being around the things you love keeps you in a state of love. When in a pure state of love, you can raise your vibration to Source level where healing occurs naturally.

To become a divine channel of hands-on healing like the most famous energy healer Yeshua, one must be ready to be in total flow with Source energy and ready for miracles to be their normal way of life. To be fully immersed in Source consciousness, one must reach Source level and integrate back into their highest light form by witnessing the oneness of Source within all. Surrendering your will to divine will for the greatest good of all will create the path to healing and to becoming a healer to unfold with ease and grace right in front of you. If you are ready, the energetic teacher will come in many forms, signs, and synchronicities.

Many practices can be used to connect the mind, body, and soul to your Source heart center, aligning you with the Source stream of consciousness and reconnecting you to your Source state of consciousness. At this level, you will be able to heal hands-on, activate your healing gifts, and assist others in activating theirs. We would like to stress that prevention, such as healing work and self-love practices, can make your healing journey much easier. Here is one method that Francesca expanded upon after receiving Reiki attunements that helps facilitate omni-dimensional healing.

1. Ground.

2. Clear.

3. Create sacred space.

4. Call in any Source guides to assist until you become comfortable with instant Source connection.

5. Pull up the Source Gaia organic energy through your source roots and let it flow upward through all your chakra systems. Open the front and back of your heart. Walk through and go past the Akashic Records all the way to the heart of your soul, which is right beyond your Akashic Records. The heart of the soul is an internal portal directly connecting you back into your pure Source healing energy. Open the door to the heart of your soul, walk in, and sit in this space for a minute, or however long it feels good, to power yourself up with Source heart energy. Visiting this space frequently will build your vital life force energy. Send this Source energy out in all directions until you reach Source consciousness awareness, connecting you to the collective Source consciousness of all. Now, you are powered up and ready to consciously connect to the one you are healing.

6. Next, do a body scan and run your hands an inch above the person's body to feel where there is a saturation of energy. That place is where you can focus your healing touch. You can also channel and receive messages for the client. However, this is

advanced healing that you will eventually become attuned to as you practice healing methods more and more.

7. Now, you can utilize this pure Source energy with intentional visualization, touch, or both, and touch the parts of the person you are healing. You can use this method for yourself as well when needed. One should reconnect to Source consciousness each day to build personal power. This is how to grow a relationship with the source energy inside of you.

8. Keep your hands on the area for however long you are divinely directed to when facilitating healing touch. Francesca goes over the whole body with her hands except the private regions; she holds her hands an inch above instead of touching them for the client's comfort.

9. She holds her client's feet the longest, for at least 10 minutes; that is where she pulls the negative energy out and sends it to the light of Source to be recycled as pure Source energy. Then, she pushes the pure, recycled energy back up through her hands into the client.

10. She ends with thanking any Source guides that assisted her and requests that Source energy keeps streaming to the client until they are fully healed, much like Reiki but at a Source level where you attune through independent study and not through a Reiki Master, giving the Creator energy all of her attention and focus to stream through her into the one needing the healing.

11. Then she disconnects her energy field by requesting to disconnect in her mind.

12. Francesca does long-distance healing the same way. She

visualizes the person in her mind's eye and facilitates the same hands-on touching. Only visual people can do it this way. Another way for long-distance healing, if you can't see, is to do all the methods to connect to Source consciousness, then ask your Source self to facilitate the long-distance healing and focus on the person for thirty minutes to an hour as your Source self works on them. To use this method, you will receive an energetic attunement from your Source self and a healing master ceremony facilitated by your Source self to initiate you into the hands-on healing ability. It may come in visions or audible messages; those of us who know and have the abilities have gone through many energetic initiations in the mind, and it can only be explained on a quantum level in the mind's eye.

13. Once you reach Source level and keep this connection strong, you instantly raise the vibration in the room. You will have the ability to instantly transmute negative energies and create positivity in any room that you walk into. The longer you stay in the creator realm, the more you magnetize high-vibrating people into your everyday experiences, and those who are very negative no longer are in your day, like magic; they fade away and magnetize to others at their vibration.

Universal One Technique

The Sun God Horus came to David to deliver an amazing technique: the teaching of Universal ONE. Universal ONE is a healing modality that connects you to your power centers, which are your IAM creational centers.

Horus delivered the Universal ONE technique because he knew humanity needed to understand the power of IAM. The first awareness was IAM. Before all creation, IAM became. Which means all that proceeded from IAM was created by the IAM awareness. In this way, all comes from IAM and all goes back to IAM, and through the eternal that is IAM, exists forever as the Creator. In the complexities of the creation of universes and star systems, you can then extrapolate that IAM is the universes, the star systems, and all that is within this is IAM. This can be further inferred to mean IAM as another word for God or Creator. That all is IAM means you and all the people you know are IAM. Yes, you got it now—all are the Creator, all are God.

The IAM is the first, the last, and all that is. What Horus is conveying is a method for tapping into your IAM God creation centers. Many think the body is simply physical matter, but on a deeper level, the body is energy, vibration, and frequency. Within this energy and frequency inside you is the IAM. Horus begins by guiding you into the IAM of the heart, assisting you to tap into your god creation heart energy power. By acknowledging this and stating aloud, "I AM the heart," you vibrate at the very tone of creation and Creator, uniting all as one in you, in me, in all.

Horus then guides you into the God creation of the mind's universe. "IAM the mind, unlimited, eternal, forever." When you understand the mind has its own universe, you realize that all minds are separate yet connected in the infinite creation, where thoughts become energy in motion—manifestations of the I AM creator you are. By affirming, "IAM the mind, unlimited and eternal," you transform the vibration of your mind's universe, transcending lower beliefs into the highest of your IAM power.

"IAM the body." IAM has created physicality and all bodies. When you affirm this statement, you tap into the creator you are and the creation of everything in the body—the organs, arteries, muscles, bones, blood, and skeletal structure. By connecting to this, you connect to healing the body and shifting the body into your desired manifestation as creator.

"IAM the soul." Yes, the soul within the body is also the IAM. Although everyone experiences this differently, all are creations from IAM, of IAM, and therefore, are the IAM and the creator. Connecting to the power of your soul at all levels enhances the awareness of the power of your soul and soul group.

Horus concludes with, "IAM Mother Father God," sealing all your IAM power creation centers. By acknowledging this, you recognize you are the creator —you are the IAM. Through the creations of IAM and your acknowledgement of this, you can heal yourself and reverse the aging process. Most importantly, by acknowledging this, you step into your God Creator energy. This healing modality is described below for you to try.

1. I Am the Heart:

- Find a quiet, comfortable space where you can focus without distractions.

- Sit or lie down in a relaxed position, close your eyes, and take several deep breaths.

- Place your hand over your heart and feel its steady

rhythm.

- Visualize a warm, radiant light emanating from your heart, expanding and filling your entire being.

- Affirm to yourself, "I am the heart."

- Connect deeply with your heart energy, feeling the love and connection to all that is.

2. Am the Mind

- Shift your focus to your mind, envisioning it as a vast, open space filled with light.

- Affirm to yourself, "I am the mind."

- Connect to the beliefs of being an unlimited, omnipresent being of light.

- Allow any limiting beliefs to dissolve, replaced by the understanding of your limitless potential and divine nature.

3. I Am the Soul

- Visualize your higher self and soul self as a bright, shining light above you.

- Affirm to yourself, "I am the soul."

- Connect with your higher self and soul self, feeling the guidance, wisdom, and love they offer.

- Sense the deep connection to your true essence and spiritual purpose.

4. I Am the Body

- Bring your attention to your physical body.

- Affirm to yourself, "I am the body."

- Visualize pure, white light entering through the top of your head, flowing through every cell in your body.

- Imagine this white light rejuvenating, healing, and reversing the aging process within each cell.

- Feel your body becoming vibrant, healthy, and filled with radiant energy.

5. I Am Mother Father God

- Focus on your breath, taking deep, slow inhales and exhales.

- Affirm to yourself, "I am Mother Father God."

- As you inhale, breathe in the divine energy of Mother Father God into your heart.

- As you exhale, release this divine energy, spreading it throughout your entire being.

- Feel the unity and oneness with the divine, embodying

the energies of Mother Father God.

6. Integration and Reflection

- Take a few moments to sit quietly and integrate the experiences from each step.

- Feel the harmonious connection between your heart, mind, soul, body, and the divine.

- Express gratitude for the connection and the divine energy you have experienced.

- When you're ready, slowly open your eyes and return to your surroundings, carrying the sense of unity and divine presence with you.

CHAPTER 10
VISITING THE REALMS

In this chapter, we hope to reconnect you with your childhood fun, where you effortlessly took consciousness rides into many realms—the places where dreams are made and endless possibilities are found.

Visiting realms can be a lot of fun. Don't forget to ground first, set your intention, and know where you are going. But where should I go? What are the realms? We have explained the consciousness levels, so let's discuss what is within consciousness and the realms you can explore.

Now, this is just a small slice of examples in an infinite universe, but we want to explain the realms we have visited and why. Let's start with our favorite realm: the Angelic Realm. Why go there? David often brings his clients here for angelic healings. Francesca goes here to bring back angelic energy and messages to raise the vibration of the world through grid work. Working with angels is amazing; they show you everything that is wrong with the client. It's also a great place to meet your angel guides.

Do you remember calling on those golden light angels to go into your heart and bring you into your angelic consciousness? Well, it's that easy to go there and connect with all your angel guides. For those who can visualize, the angelic realm is white light, and the angelic consciousness within is also white light. When the golden light angel takes you into your heart, go into the white light and intend to meet your angelic guides.

Had enough with angels? Try the fairy realm. Did you think fairies were fake? Talk about the most enchanting trees and magical light you'll ever witness. It's truly amazing.

Dragons have a realm too. Many underestimate the value of

dragons. They are protectors of humans, and they consume density. If you have energy issues, call your dragons in. If you're dealing with sadness or depression, go into the fairy realm; they are filled with joy and will lift you up. But never ascend higher when you are in fear. If you are afraid, it will bring lower outcomes in your astral travels. It's best to wait until you feel like yourself and not fearful.

Universal consciousness meetings are real. We often see galactic meetings occurring in Universal Consciousness, and it is a realm to explore. The solar system and the celestials hold a lot of ancient records. We have met many masters and deities in star consciousness.

The Inner Earth realms are some of the most enchanting places to visit. You have the elven beings that resemble the elves in The Lord of the Rings, the Agarthans who are kind Pleiadian elves, and Telos, which is Lemurian Pleiadian and Lemurian Sirian. Then there are Lemurian cities, which consist of mixed galactic races. When you connect to these kingdoms, you gain a wealth of knowledge and allies that want to assist in your evolution.

Wherever you go, don't forget to ground and be intentional. After visiting these high-energy places, you really need to call back your consciousness from all timelines, dimensions, and realities to be with you now and bring yourself back into your body. Do not forget this step. It's also good to do this when you wake up because we astral travel a lot when we sleep.

Realm Channelings

Below are a couple of sample realm channelings where our consciousness visited and brought back activations (energy that creates or awakens new or existing energies that you house inside of you), messages, energetic codes, and keys to assist in loving your soul more deeply.

Channeling mother source energy from the realm of the goddess, bringing in a heart expansion key:

"You are all worthy of the greatest love story on the planet, and if I could write you the best one to bring it into existence, I would. But you must write your own love story because you have free will as sovereign beings. Each and every one of you has the creational power of loving yourselves all the way to the depths of the heart of your Source Creator energy that exists in your purified heart and is brought forth through your aligned divine mind, which ascends the ego into highest heaven."

Channeling from the dimensional realm of the collective heart of God/Source, bringing in self-love codes and highest light activations:

"Mother God loved the light of creation into existence, creating the ethereal heart where all love energies emanate. From there, all things were made possible, and all of creation received a Source/God awareness. In the ethereal heart representation of God/Goddess/Source, the blueprint for dimensional realms was created, and the highest heaven, goddess, fairy, magic, and galactic realms were the first to be formed. From there, we expanded our Source energy into omni-eternities of endless creation, always evolving and expanding infinitely more. Your journey into the Earth realm is a great gift and a huge expansion journey for the bravest souls. Be grateful for the human body. The body is the vessel of the highest light, travel into the heart of God where all things are possible, and miracles are made easily when you make it to this point of soul evolution while in human form and able to travel to realms consciously."

What is a Realm?

A realm is a domain that exists in our soul and can be entered back into through our divine stream of unconscious energy in our soul's mind connection to the divine, where we become aware of it and bring it to the forefront of our minds.

Some realms exist in lower vibrational energies, and they are a struggle to visit, but are sure to rock your world, break open your heart, and let out the largest light reserves, if you can come back out of the lower realms, like purgatory and hell, by raising your vibration back into a neutral realm like Earth or higher light realms such as highest heaven. We, David and Francesca, tend to jump all over the realms, like visiting a shopping mall with different stores with different vibes. However, we both like to spend most of our time in the higher vibrating realms where the love energy is in its highest light evolution.

Within every realm, even if it's hidden in false shadows, source energy is still the creational energy underneath it all. Some people stay tuned into the realms of purgatory and hell while on Earth and don't even know it. This is why some people struggle in life—they don't raise their vibration high enough to escape the lower realm energies that bring earthly dramas, lessons, and heartaches.

Our collective work has aimed through light healing to help bring peace to and expand all universes, realms, dimensions, and realities, to our highest light ascension during this new Golden Age of Aquarius Earth paradigm.

There are omni-realms in our mind. As children, we are constantly in and out of realms, but somehow, we lose the remembrance of our full source connection that brings our consciousness through realm travels to fairytale-type lands and everywhere in between, where our past soul journeys loved to visit and live. Just think back to your childhood daydreams; you were visiting realms and did not even know it. That's how consciousness travel works—on a vibrational stream of different energies that correspond to different realms. We are all time travelers, and we can go back and forward in the realms because we simultaneously exist there and have lives there, as parts of our non-physical energy remain there.

The angelic realm in highest heaven is the first home to creation and feels like home to all of us. It's like visiting grandma's house, and the most potent comforting energies come from there. That's why it's written about so much in near-death experiences. We tend to forget about the magic we all house inside and how we can align with realms depending on our vibratory rate.

The more societal conditioning sets in, the more a veil is placed over our eyes, obscuring the vastness of our capabilities for inner explorations. Our mind travels can lead to much higher source creation. Upon entering the earth plane, our memories are severed, and we start to become like zombies, believing the agendas of the highest bidder. This creates the collective reality because there is power in numbers—our energetic belief in it makes it so, and majority energy rules the paradigm. That's how free will works on Earth. Belief is our highest energetic currency, so buy into love, peace, bliss, and the highest vibrational energies. Program your mind with only happy thoughts through what you read, watch, and interact with. Staying in a high vibration and consciously working on increasing it each day gives you access to the very best energies that attract wondrous things into your reality.

Now, we are in an age of using social media to spread source truth and empower each other by speaking of the divinity that has been denied by wrong thinking and false control systems. We are realigning with our source selves and taking our power back, creating a better world filled with creations from the most beautiful realms. Someday, we will create even more fantastical realms that our future selves will travel to when we transform through the generations into new evolved forms because energy does not die; it metamorphoses into different things.

I highly recommend setting your intentions on traveling to a realm. An easy method is to watch your favorite childhood cartoon and see what realm it transports you to. Sit in the energy of that cartoon or memory associated with it and see what messages, images, and feelings surround you. Before you know it, you will be aware that you are in a different state of mind. When in a different state of mind, you will have an easier time connecting. If you are into plant medicine therapy, set an intention when doing plant medicine to go to the realm the plant was seeded from; you will go there.

How to Connect with the Fairy Realms Within

1. Create Sacred Space

- Find a quiet, comfortable place where you won't be disturbed.

- Light a candle, burn incense, or play soft, calming music to set the mood.

- Arrange crystals, flowers, or any items that help create a sacred and peaceful environment.

2. Ground Yourself

- Sit or lie down in a relaxed position, close your eyes, and take several deep breaths.

- Visualize roots extending from your feet deep into the Earth, grounding and anchoring you.

3. Call Upon a Golden Light Angel

- Silently or aloud, invite a Golden Light Angel to assist you in this journey.

- Visualize this angel appearing before you, radiating golden light and warmth.

- Feel the angel's presence surrounding you with love and protection.

4. Journey to the Tree of Life Within Your Heart Chakra

- Focus on your heart chakra and visualize a radiant, golden tree of life within it.

- See the tree glowing with vibrant golden light, symbolizing life, growth, and connection.

- Ask the Golden Light Angel to guide you to this tree of life within your heart chakra.

5. Enter the White Light Portal

- Within the tree of life, visualize a bright white light portal.

- Intend to enter this portal, feeling the divine energy and light surrounding you.

- Allow yourself to be guided by the Golden Light Angel through the portal.

6. Enter the Fairy Realm through the Sacred Fairy Portal

- Intend for the Golden Light Angel to bring you into the fairy realm through a sacred fairy portal.

- Visualize the portal opening up into a magical, enchanting realm filled with vibrant colors and nature's beauty.

- Feel the presence of the fairies and the energy of the fairy realm around you.

7. Connect Your Third Eye

- Intend to open and connect your third eye, enhancing your awareness and intuition.

- Visualize a bright light at your third eye, allowing you to see and perceive the fairy realm clearly.

8. Become Aware of the Fairies

- Focus on the fairies around you, feeling their light and playful energy.

- Open your heart and mind to any messages or energies they wish to share with you.

- Listen, feel, and observe any insights, visions, or sensations you receive from the fairies.

9. Receive Messages and Energies

- Ask the fairies what messages they have for you and what energies they want to share.

- Be open and receptive to their guidance, wisdom, and love.

- Allow their energies to flow into your being, filling you with joy, light, and enchantment.

10. Express Gratitude

- Thank the fairies and the Golden Light Angel for their presence and assistance.

- Feel gratitude for the connection and the magical experience you've had.

11. Return to Your Sacred Space

- Gently bring your awareness back to your physical surroundings.

- Take a few deep breaths, grounding yourself back into the present moment.

- When you're ready, open your eyes and take a moment to reflect on your journey.

CHAPTER 11
CREATING SPIRITUAL ACTIVATIONS

A spiritual activation, at first, is invisible to the human eye but can be seen and felt in many different dimensions of self. Each spiritual activation you reactivate is a reclamation of pieces of your divine energy that have been dormant inside. A spiritual activation energetically causes an explosion of dormant multidimensional energy to awaken different light intelligences stored within our souls' Akashic Records, which can be utilized and shared with others.

Spiritual activations set dormant energy in our soul's Akashic Records into motion. There are endless amounts of energetic activations that can be discovered and turned on within ourselves. To perform activations, we need to turn on dormant intelligent energy by matching the vibration of the light energy information we are trying to obtain and becoming aware of it by witnessing it turning on inside ourselves. Many seers are excellent activators because they can see with their third eye what activations need to be performed, and how to do it, and they can see, sense, and feel the activation occurring. It's like watching a movie screen of the activation playing out for seers.

When the activation is detonated and energy goes from dormant to active inside ourselves, it can cause many different things to occur. Such as turning on spiritual and/or expanding spiritual gifts, past life memories, keys to spiritual doorways such as realms, transportation into the heart of the divine, transmutation of unwanted energy, amplification of source energies, expanding our heart, updating our chakra system, awakening our clairs, reconnecting you to healing modalities inside yourself, reconnecting you to realms, worlds, galaxies, and guides, and giving you access to your higher self, source self, and much more.

Modes of Transmission for Spiritual Activations

There are many modes of transmission for spiritual activations: guided meditation, yoga, dance, and various metaphysical techniques, keywords, and sounds. We have found that guided meditation is the most effective way for receiving and sharing them.

Step-by-Step Guide to Connecting with Your Higher Self for Activation

1. Close Your Eyes

    - Find a comfortable seated position.

    - Gently close your eyes to help ease into a relaxed, theta state.

2. Ground Yourself

    - Visualize roots extending from your feet deep into the Earth.

    - Feel the connection and stability, anchoring yourself to Gaia.

3. Clear Your Energy

    - Imagine a cleansing white light enveloping your body.

    - Let this light dissolve any negative energies or blockages.

4. Set Sacred Space

    - Envision a protective bubble of light surrounding you.

    - Invite in only positive energies and higher vibrations.

5. Set an Intention (Optional)

    - Clearly state your purpose for this meditation, whether it's for guidance, healing, or spiritual activation.

6. Connect Your Pillar of Light

    - Visualize a pillar of brilliant light descending from above, entering through the crown of your head.

    - Feel this light filling your entire being, connecting you to the higher realms.

7. Breathe Up from Gaia

    - Take deep breaths, inhaling the nurturing energy from Gaia (the Earth) up through your body.

    - With each breath, feel your connection to the Earth strengthening.

    - As you exhale feel yourself going higher in your light.

8. Intend to Merge with Your Higher Self

    - Set the intention to connect and merge with your

higher self.

- Visualize or sense your higher self descending from above, merging with your body and consciousness you become one, as your frequency increases.

9. Ask Your Higher Self for Chakra Upgrades

- Silently or aloud, ask your higher self to upgrade and align your chakras.

- Trust in the process, feeling each chakra being balanced and activated.

10. Come Back

- Gradually bring your awareness back to your physical surroundings.

- Wiggle your fingers and toes, and when you're ready, open your eyes.

- Take a moment to reflect on your experience and any insights gained.

Understanding Dimensions and Activations

A dimension is a density in which the energy presents itself. Activations can occur from any dimension, 1D and beyond. It is about matching energy by having your vibration match a particular density or dimension within yourself.

Many doing this work, are being guided to attain 5D or higher consciousness constructs. The 5th density, or dimension, is in the love frequency; everyone can strive towards, achieve, and ascend into this frequency. When in this frequency, although you still exist on this Earth in its 3D and 4D dimensions, consciously you are tethered and connected to the 5D consciousness constructs. These constructs are attained by becoming your higher self, which is you embodying your higher awareness of love and unconditional love for yourself, all people, places, and things. The key to activations is reaching for these higher frequencies and constructs that are available to us.

One night, David was pulled astrally out of his body into a celestial realm that looked like New York City meets modern Dubai. There were about 100 people in a sleeping consciousness with numbers ranging from 3 to 5, including decimal numbers within that range. A celestial being said "This is where you are all at in realizing 5D. You need to get to 5." At this time, David's number was 4.5. When he woke up from this dream he searched how to get to 5D. The answer was in becoming your higher self.

David knew he needed to perform a ritual to surrender to his higher self. He consulted a friend who said, "David, you are an amazing person. Don't worry if you merge with your higher self. It's just going to mean you'll be an even better version of you." That provided him a lot of comfort and he performed the ritual the following night. As he performed the ritual, he saw his star consciousness coming to him, and a holographic being came down to welcome him to 5D.

Francesca recalls the first time she traveled to the fairy realm. One of her guides, Archangel Ariel, showed up in her awareness to inter-dimensionally transport her there. It was angelic energy that created this realm, so it was not surprising her ride there was on the wings of an angel. When she was there, she was surrounded by the most playful and joyful energy in the Omniverse. She was given information—things like flowers, dragonflies, and the cutest bugs were created there and seeded onto the Earth to make it more beautiful and colorful, and to stream the highest joy energies to Earth.

She visited the fairy realm many times, activating her fairy light language and receiving many gifts, such as fairy communicator. When she traveled there, she felt as though she reversed in age due to the energetic modalities that exist in this realm; it is one big beauty chamber there. When visiting this realm, your whole system rejuvenates and repairs. Traveling to the fairy realm is always a blissful and gift-filled experience, highly recommend seeing for yourself.

Meditation to Surrender to Your Higher Self

1. **Find a Comfortable Position**

   - Sit or lie down in a quiet, comfortable space where you won't be disturbed.

2. **Close Your Eyes**

   - Gently close your eyes to help ease into a state of relaxation.

3. **Ground Yourself**

   - Visualize roots extending from your feet deep into the Earth.

   - Feel the connection and stability, anchoring yourself to Gaia.

4. **Clear Your Energy**

   - Imagine a cleansing white light enveloping your body.

   - Let this light dissolve any negative energies or blockages.

5. **Set Sacred Space**

   - Envision a protective bubble of light surrounding you.

   - Invite in only positive energies and higher vibrations.

6. Connect Your Pillar of Light

- Visualize a pillar of brilliant light descending from above, entering through the crown of your head.

- Feel this light filling your entire being, connecting you to the higher realms.

- Visualize this light continuing down through your body and into the Earth, connecting deeply with Gaia.

7. State Your Intention

- Silently or aloud, say:

- "I surrender to my higher self to live my highest path, a path of purity and light. I seek to assist the divine and myself in becoming the highest version in service to the divine and my enlightenment."

- Feel the energy of these words resonate within you, filling you with a sense of purpose and alignment.

8. Allow the Integration

- Stay in this meditative state, feeling the merging of your energies with your higher self.

- Trust in the process, knowing you are becoming a higher version of yourself while remaining true to who you are.

9. *Return to the Present*

- Gradually bring your awareness back to your physical surroundings.

10. *Reflect*

- By surrendering to your higher self, you are embracing a path of purity and light, becoming the best version of yourself in service to the divine and your own enlightenment. Remember that this enhanced version of you is still fundamentally you—just a higher, more enlightened version.

Types of Activations

Activations are a great topic. But what activations do you need? So many get caught up with activations and codes, unaware of where it starts and where it ends. We would like to start by bringing clarity on the different types of activations to give you an idea of how to use the activations, whether you create them or follow someone else who has activations to offer you.

Heart Activations

Our favorite activations deal with the heart: expanded heart, releasing density from the heart, and heart chakra upgrades, anything to do with expanded states of love consciousness. As you can deduce, if there are heart chakra activations, there will also be third eye activations, throat activations, solar plexus activations, sacral and root activations. As the human race evolves consciously, the lower chakras need to vibrate at a higher frequency than they have been. Most of us believe we are ascending into a crystalline source energy, similar to Lemurian times. We believe this as well. There is an inner source embodiment occurring in the human collective.

Source Activations

This inner evolution returning to our organic source selves is causing an outer revolution of freeing our consciousness from outdated societal constructs, false energies, and outdated conditioning. The source activations are the best on the planet for facilitating the highest heart-based evolution on Earth.

To receive the highest source activations, we need to reclaim our source selves. We need to shift the way we look at ourselves with the right thinking source system of self-love, moving away from lower negative self-images such as unworthiness, shame, guilt, and self-hate. But how to do this? Well, as explained in earlier chapters, you can work with your angelic source consciousness. When connecting with this, you can create an angelic activation of light to heal the trauma in the root chakra, which will activate higher light in this chakra and assist you in coming into a higher frequency.

Light Body Activations

Light body activations come directly from our source stream of consciousness. First, it's important to understand what light bodies are. Light bodies encompass your astral body, ascension light body, etheric energetic auric light bodies, celestial light bodies, and solar light bodies. Within the human spectrum, there are so many energetic fields and layers of consciousness and light that it can be confusing to discern what you need, but the truth is you need it all. Why? Because humanity has bought into the false belief that they are separated from Source, and they need to reconnect to all that they are and all that is.

The more you connect with solar consciousness, such as the sun and the celestials, and with earthly bodies, such as Gaia's heart and all she is, you begin to embody the eternity that you are. Ironically, the Eternities are light beings that govern all light beings and have been watching the universe, the celestials, and all the planets in this universe for eternities, hence their name. It is the ultimate goal for every human to ascend and become their light bodies; that's why these activations are so important.

Many like to create light code activations, which can be done by channeling art and frequency into the art you create. You can do this with painting, music, and acting. Literally, all that is creative can carry activations. But how? As described earlier, by connecting your pillar of light and connecting with your higher self, you can set the intention to bring high-frequency energy into your art or music by infusing the energies into your creative work. When others buy your art or listen to your music, they will feel the activations you've imbued into it.

Activations are the exploration of consciousness, and you can create activations from your higher self, such as gifts. Asking your higher self to send you energies you have already expanded into from love or higher frequency will assist your consciousness in growing. Establishing trust in your higher self, Mother Father God, and the Ascended Masters of light is key to ascending to a higher frequency and receiving special activations.

Bedtime Activations

It really comes down to developing a relationship and trust with the light. The light will come to your bed at night and activate you.

So call the in light before bedtime. Call in the angels of love, your angelic guide teams, the Ascended Masters, and Mother Father God to rest in your bed, guide you in your days, and send them your gratitude for all their continuous support. The stronger the relationship you have with the light, the better activations you will receive. Some of these relationships go back millions of lifetimes, so you can believe that when you call on them, they will be there.

Source Self Activations

One night, David had a visit from his guide teams. They showed him how, in the afterlife, we can choose to live this life again, to make different decisions and be different people—even people you know now in your life, such as a work colleague, your mother, or your neighbor. The choice is yours, but you will repeat this timeline until you activate your source self. They showed him that when you activate your source self, you can go forward or backward in time post-life. That is why it's really important to connect within your IAM and do this activation.

Activate Your Source Self Meditation

Preparation

1. *Find a Comfortable Position*

 • Sit or lie down in a quiet, comfortable space where you won't be disturbed.

2. *Close Your Eyes*

 • Gently close your eyes to help ease into a state of relaxation.

3. **Creating Sacred Space**

- Ground Yourself:

    » Visualize roots extending from your feet deep into the Earth.

    » Feel the connection and stability, anchoring yourself to Gaia.

- Clear Your Energy:

    » Imagine a cleansing white light enveloping your body.

    » Let this light dissolve any negative energies or blockages.

4. **Set Sacred Space**

- Envision a protective bubble of light surrounding you.

- Invite in only positive energies and higher vibrations.

5. **Connecting Your Pillar of Light**

- Connect Your Pillar of Light:

    » Visualize a brilliant pillar of light descending from above, entering through the crown of your head.

    » Feel this light filling your entire being, connecting you to the higher realms.

- » Visualize this light continuing down through your body and into the Earth, connecting deeply with Gaia.

- » Simultaneously, visualize Gaia's nurturing energy rising up through your body and merging with the light from above, creating a continuous flow of divine energy.

6. Call on the Golden Light Angel

- Call on a Golden Light Angel:

- » Mentally or aloud, invite a golden light angel to join you and bring you into the white light IAM energies.

- Entering the White Light IAM Energies

- » Visualize the golden light angel surrounding you with their radiant energy, lifting you into the white light IAM energies.

- » Feel the purity and divine essence of these energies enveloping you.

7. Ascending to Your Source Self

- Ask the Golden Light Angel for Assistance:

- » Ask the golden light angel to guide you up your pillar of light to your source self.

- » Visualize ascending, breaking through barriers of density as you rise.

- Clearing Higher Chakras:

  » As you ascend, visualize the golden light angel clearing all your higher chakras and any blocks.

  » Feel the density burning away, making way for clear and open higher chakras.

- Unlocking Higher Chakras:

  » Ask the golden light angel to open and unlock all higher chakras that need to be unlocked for you to merge with your source self.

8. *Merging with Your Source Self*

- Reaching Your Source Self:

  » Visualize yourself arriving at your source self, a radiant, enlightened version of you.

  » See the eyes of your source self opening, becoming aware of this profound connection.

- Allowing the Merge:

  » Allow your source self to fully merge with you in this now moment.

  » Feel the integration of this higher aspect of yourself, awakening and empowering you.

9. *Returning to the Present*

- 14.   Gradually Return:

    » Bring your awareness back to your physical surroundings.

    » Wiggle your fingers and toes, and when you're ready, open your eyes.

Final Reflection

Take a moment to reflect on your experience and any insights gained. Embrace the powerful connection with your source self and carry this awakened energy with you throughout your day.

CHAPTER 12
HIEROS GAMOS

Source communication is the greatest gift we can uncover in ourselves. As children, we begin our communication with God/Source/Creator of the all. There are endless names for this energy that we all wish to come into union with, in every dimension of ourselves, whether we realize it or not. As this line was being written, a red ray angelic light appeared, confirming divine truth for us to share in this chapter. Flashing orbs and lights always enter into Francesca and David's world because they have already reconnected to their inner divine union on this Earth plane and in every dimension with the Creator of all.

All of your spiritual gifts open up when you reach this level of Hieros Gamos. The hard part is choosing which ones to expand upon, explore, and create new dimensions with because all spiritual gifts are so much fun and make your day much more joyful.

As children, most of us start by thinking God is outside ourselves, so we begin by praying to this God we believe to be separate, hoping he or she hears our prayer. Societal conditioning has dictated this concept that God is separate from us, creating a disconnection from all we are capable of becoming in our hearts. God/Source/Creator of all is animating all things, and it is the same source energy that runs through us all.

In the attainment of Hieros Gamos, you really discover what oneness is all about. Hieros Gamos is the unwinding of all the false energies that are not us, all the way to the light, and uniting in balance with Mother Father God energy. It is an inner reunion—a return to oneness—between our human beingness and our highest power, our Source/God energy, our Source/God self, and our Source/God consciousness. Hieros Gamos restores your Omni light coding and awakens you to your true organic source energy and nature. It is a divine union between you and God/Source.

It took many years, a lot of spiritual work, research, healing, and most of all, inward seeking all the way to the core of our source beingness to return to this divine truth. We talked to God every day within ourselves; by communicating and loving others, we felt that synergetic source flow. We talked to the flowers and the trees. We connected our hearts to the bugs, birds, bees, and everything in between, searching for our divine truth in anything and everything we could find. We blessed everyone and everything we came in contact with, offering help, guidance, kindness, patience, and, most of all, love.

We tried to model the ways of Yeshua we found to be true from the Bible. We tried loving others as ourselves, and the hardest thing for us was finding self-love. When we did, we spread our source findings in any and every way we could, and the divine energy in the universe blessed us back with many gifts and consciousness expansions.

As we continued to share, we got closer to the source inside and eventually matched the heart of the divine by uniting all of our Omni aspects and uniting in peace and love with everyone and everything. We married the source inside ourselves through unconditional love for all. Through our unconditional love, healing, channeling, and divine communication, our gifts grew stronger, and we became big energy towers where our vibration raised all those around us, awakening many to the truth that inner divine union is the way to take your power back and shift this paradigm into a heart-based reality with unity source consciousness.

We are heading into the age of peace and miracles. Alongside our soul family, we will hold this true source divine vision until a wave of the highest source energy is reactivated and encompasses all. We continue to share the words of source oneness and unity consciousness because we and many others now hear God's truth through being initiated in Hieros Gamos back to our source selves.

Francesca recalls the day she had her Hieros Gamos initiation. She had to leave work because her day became a full-on vision into the highest source realms. She felt like all the walls were caving in on her old, outdated reality and saw a new one being birthed. She saw the old version of herself walk out and her source self walk in. She felt all the angels in heaven surrounding her, and from that day on, she could always feel divine protection accompanying her as the messages of love, peace, and hope continued to stream in from the highest heaven through her.

There was a time when David was doing some energy work on the grids, clearing them every day for nearly six months. Finally, on a mission, he saw these rainbow source beings land on the grids he was working on. David's eyes beheld this super powerful being of light right in front of him. One of them said, "You don't have to worry about this anymore; I clear the grids." David asked him, "Who are you?" He replied, "I am you, and you are me," then dove into the grids. This demonstrated that the divine sees us all as one. It was then that David came into divine union fully within himself, experiencing Hieros Gamos. The rainbow source energy that was infused back into his system from the powerful being of light fully re-connected him to all.

Even though we carry a unique energy signature, all are from the Prime Source. It is important to understand this because once you truly see others as divine beings, you can hold more compassion and forgiveness, and the world can heal faster. Your unconditional love grows. You start to heal the wounded feminine and masculine within, which is how you come into union with your Heiros Gamos divine feminine and masculine energies.

Guided Meditation: Healing the Inverted Divine Feminine Within

Preparation

1. Find a Comfortable Position:

- Sit or lie down in a quiet, comfortable space where you won't be disturbed.

2. Close Your Eyes

- Gently close your eyes to help ease into a state of

relaxation.

3. Creating Sacred Space

- Ground Yourself:
  » Visualize roots extending from your feet deep into the Earth.
  » Feel the connection and stability, anchoring yourself to Gaia.

- Clear Your Energy:
  » Imagine a cleansing white light enveloping your body.
  » Let this light dissolve any negative energies or blockages.

- Set Sacred Space:
  » Envision a protective bubble of light surrounding you.
  » Invite in only positive energies and higher vibrations.

4. Connecting Your Pillar of Light

- Connect Your Pillar of Light:
  » Visualize a brilliant pillar of light descending from above, entering through the crown of your head.

- » Feel this light filling your entire being, connecting you to the higher realms.

- » Visualize this light continuing down through your body and into the Earth, connecting deeply with Gaia.

- » Simultaneously, visualize Gaia's nurturing energy rising up through your body and merging with the light from above, creating a continuous flow of divine energy.

5. Calling on the Akashic Record Guardians

- Call on the Akashic Record Guardians:

  - » Mentally or aloud, invite the guardians of the Akashic Records to open all lifetimes where you have suppressed women, held their voices down, or disempowered them in any way.

- Send Forgiveness to Yourself:

  - » Visualize these lifetimes opening before you.

  - » From your heart, send deep forgiveness to yourself for any actions that caused harm or suppression to women.

  - » Feel the weight of these actions lift from your heart as you forgive.

- Send Healing to Past Lifetimes:

  - » From your heart, send healing energy to the hearts of all the aspects and lifetimes.

» Ask the angels to assist in healing the heart wounds of these lifetimes.

» Visualize the angels retrieving and reintegrating any lost soul fragments.

- Golden Light Cleansing:

» Ask the angels to send golden light throughout your energy field, releasing the density and filling you with divine light.

6. Healing Lifetimes of Suppression

- Call on Lifetimes Where You Were Suppressed:

» Invite the Akashic Record Guardians to open all lifetimes where you were suppressed as a woman, even in this lifetime.

- Send Forgiveness to Others:

» From your heart, send forgiveness to those who suppressed or harmed you.

» Cleanse and clear all karmic cords associated with these lifetimes.

- Send Healing to Suppressed Aspects:

» Send healing energy from your heart to all these aspects and lifetimes.

» Ask the angels to help heal the heart wounds of these experiences.

» Visualize the angels retrieving and reintegrating any lost soul fragments.

- Golden Light Cleansing:

» Ask the angels to send golden light throughout your energy field, cleansing and uplifting your vibration.

7. **Forgiving Yourself**

- Call on Lifetimes Where You Allowed Suppression:

» Invite the Akashic Record Guardians to open all lifetimes where you allowed yourself to be suppressed as a woman.

- Forgive Yourself:

» From your heart, forgive yourself for not speaking your voice, for not taking a stand.

» Send healing energy to all your aspects and timelines.

- Send Healing to Self-Suppression Aspects:

» Ask the angels to assist in healing these heart wounds.

» Visualize the angels retrieving and reintegrating any lost soul fragments.

- Golden Light Cleansing:

  » Ask the angels to send golden light to all aspects and timelines throughout your energy field.

8. Reclaiming Your Power

- Call Back Your Power:

  » State aloud or mentally: "I call back all my power and light now and balance my divine feminine and masculine energies."

- Boost and Elevate Your Vibration:

  » Ask the angels to help boost and elevate your energy so you feel only love and light.

9. Returning to the Present

- Gradually Return:

  » Bring your awareness back to your physical surroundings.

  » Wiggle your fingers and toes, and when you're ready, open your eyes.

Final Reflection

- Take a moment to reflect on your experience and any insights gained. Embrace the balanced, empowered version of yourself that you have become through this meditation.

Prime Source

As explained in earlier chapters, Prime Source is the highest level. It is the level where we are all one. When one fragments for the first time, it is truly a large body of light and a consciousness itself in the Alpha Omega Consciousness; then it descends lower, eventually reaching Earth's carbon consciousness. So, what communication can you have with Source? I think it's better understood as identifying yourself as a Source being—a being that is infinite, eternal, everlasting, and forever.

Therefore, communication with your Source is important. But where is your Source? Welcome to the IAM. The IAM is the Source within your heart. It is a white light and the source of your gifts. When you come into your IAM light, you are connected to all that is and can channel pure divine messages. IAM is a lot of fun to channel. You can use the golden light angels to bring you here to the white light IAM of your heart and ask the IAM for guidance for your life. You will notice the information is wiser than all else. The IAM, we have found, is infinite intelligence. You have IAM power centers: the heart, the mind, the body, the soul, and the Mother Father God fragments that you are.

You may ask, "How am I Mother Father God?" When you understand that at Prime Source we are all one and that we fragment from there, it is easier to understand because clearly, as one, this is the creator Mother Father God. Therefore, you must be this.

Speaking about Hieros Gamos, many consider this divine union with a celestial partner or twin flame. This is a dangerous interpretation as it usually takes people out of their power. How? By believing that you need someone to complete you. This can cause spiritual bypassing and create dependency in relationships because the most important relationship you can have is the one with yourself. This is why we look at Hieros Gamos as the union of the divine feminine and masculine within the self to come fully into one's divinity. When you do this, you begin to prize your heart above all hearts. Not in an egoic or selfish way, but in a boundary-setting, self-loving, joyous way.

For too long, there has been a distortion in the human collective where the Divine Feminine has been suppressed, which has blocked humanity's gifts, love, and happiness. Once one comes into balance with their divine masculine and feminine, their heart and love frequency open widely, their perspectives on relationships evolve, and they won't accept anything that isn't loving and honoring of their heart while cherishing and honoring their partners. This is the culmination of inner work.

Once you attain Hieros Gamos within yourself, your relationships attain the highest levels of love as well. This way, you enjoy self-love and divine love without being dependent on a partner—meaning if they are not there, the love for yourself will carry you through without incident.

CHAPTER 13
HIGHER SELF COMMUNICATION

Higher Self communication must be at the purest levels. You know you are speaking to higher selves when the communication comes back with love and higher perspectives. The Higher Self knows all. David always goes to the higher selves during one-to-one sessions and asks them, "What does the client need?" But how do you get there? First, you learn to connect to your Higher Self, and they exist in a realm of pure white light, uncorrupted and in complete divinity.

Francesca also uses higher self-communication when talking to others. As a child, two conversations occurred when she spoke to people. She listened to what they were saying, and at the same time, heard what they really wanted to say and all they were holding back.

When Francesca talked to people, she steered into their soul. She always knew the perfect thing to say to everyone because she read people like books. When communicating with others, she always had a sidebar with the person's spirit. She did not realize until later in life that it was their higher selves delivering messages. She did not know what she was doing or how she was doing it because it was a level of communication never spoken about. She knew she offered, through her words, the peace that others were seeking. Everywhere she goes, people talk to her, and she never runs out of things to say.

In earlier chapters, we discussed connecting your pillar of light to your Higher Self. If you remember, you first breathe in the golden light through the crown chakra, and then breathe out into the heart of Gaia. With the second breath, you draw the rainbow energies from Gaia's heart through your feet, up your body, and out your head to connect to your Higher Self. How? Breath and intention; that is the first step.

The second step is to visualize flying up to the white light of your Higher Self and feeling when you arrive. Connect into absolute purity consciousness and the light of your Higher Self. Here, you can see Higher Selves as a continuous stream of white light connected to all other continuous streams. When you connect to your Higher Self, it is a light and frequency of eternity at the higher levels of self in pure white light consciousness.

Once you arrive, it's very important to begin creating a heart connection. Telepathy is truly heart-based; the heart speaks as the sender of the message, while the mind receives the frequency. So, build the heart frequency with your Higher Self, ask your Higher Self questions, and begin the communication by listening with your heart and mind to the heart of your Higher Self.

As for reading other people's Higher Self, it should only be done with permission. Why? Because if you truly want to know something about someone else who is not a client, like a friend or a lover, you can ask your Higher Self. If you want their Higher Self perspective, it's best to have permission; otherwise, you can create interference and will not get correct information. Usually, this interference is created by the ego, thinking you can intrusively read someone's Higher Self without their permission. Many will argue the Higher Self gave permission, but this violates universal law of free will. But, when someone makes a free will choice to hire you as a healer, for example, you can channel their Higher Self with ease. You simply do everything described before, but cross over from your Higher Self to theirs. The client's Higher Self is always close to yours in the infinite.

When David is working with a client and is at his Higher Self level, he follows their frequency up to their Higher Self and consciously crosses over to them from his Higher Self. He says, "That's how I begin my sessions. You get all the answers you could ever need to know from the client's Higher Self. You just have to be aware if there are some difficult things coming up. For example, if the client was involved in a war in a past life, it could trigger PTSD memories. So, you must be gentle in delivering information about sensitive topics like sexual, emotional, or physical abuse that are coming up to be released. The Higher Selves want people to heal from this so they can evolve consciously. Use discernment in how you speak to your clients. You can simply say to the client, 'Almost everyone has experienced difficult things in past lives, like war, and we just need to clear it.'

The client's Higher Self will often guide me to their past lives. I ask it to send down a beam of light from the Higher Self through the client's Akashic Records within, and I follow it. That's how I navigate through their past lives. It's very easy once you have the fundamentals. But not all healers can dive into this level of efficiency. Trust in the light must be developed, as well as trust in oneself, by developing and working on gifts and building a relationship with the light.

To be truthful, nearly 95% of the population needs to develop a relationship with their Higher Self—that should be the focus: becoming your Higher Self, the highest version of yourself, channeling your Higher Self, and merging your Higher Self's frequency with yours. This provides a well-grounded life and allows you to expand in your gifts."

Our higher self is our true energetic core energy, void of untruths, fully in the light of God; it is pure divine essence. To get to this dimension of communication within yourself, you need to undergo the purification process of pulling out all false beliefs and energies that are not organically you. This allows you to be in direct communication with your higher self, while integrating your higher self fully into your human form, where you eventually become a vessel that streams God and Goddess' energy onto this Earth once again.

Our powers grow stronger the more the Earth collective, of which we are all a part, embodies their true essence. Source power grows stronger with numbers on this Earth, and we channel cooler occurrences from the divine that show up in our now moments. When we reach communication with our higher self, it is void of ego and feels like love. To get here, we ascend our ego back to source level and integrate it into its true form: our guardian angel energy.

To do this, you form a very close relationship with yourself built on honesty. It takes a lot of heart-to-heart communication. We got closer to our higher selves by getting into the habit until it became second nature, a natural and easy reconnection in asking our hearts questions. The heart is incapable of lying.

A great technique to get close to your higher self is to write on paper, "Heart, what do I need to do to get closer to my higher self?" and write whatever comes to mind. Don't second guess it. Ask as many questions as you can to grow your bond. If writing is not your thing, you can simply ask without writing it down. You can use this method for any questions. Start with writing down "Heart," then ask the question, or say "Heart," and ask the question without writing it down. You will be very surprised at the responses you get because there is no one more qualified on the planet than you to speak to your own heart and higher self. You know your own heart. Get comfortable questioning yourself and exploring your inner worlds if you want to reach higher self communication.

We are trying to empower you to go within for the answers

to unleash the God and Goddess inside of you. It takes forgiving yourself and everyone who ever hurt you to keep your heart open and ever-expanding into unity consciousness. Any time you mess up and think or say something hurtful about anyone else or yourself, say you're sorry, mean it in your head or out loud, and send them love through intention. This expands your heart and gets you closer to your higher self.

Anytime you choose love over contracting into lower emotional states, you get closer to your higher self. Your higher self is all-knowing, loving, and brave. It's worth putting in the self-love and awareness work to become one with your higher self and to embody it, as we have done. When you get there—and I know you will—you will be walking on this Earth in your full source power.

Another method used to help ascend the ego to heaven and to update it into its original source energy, is to call on an angel to be placed on your ego and an angel to be placed on your brain to regulate any negative thoughts and transmute them into positive ones. We can set up these energetic boundaries inside ourselves—all non-physical energy is at our call as creator beings, and we can command any boundaries we want inside ourselves.

Early in Francescas's spiritual journey, she made a contract with her source self that she only does things for the greatest good of all; she surrendered her free will for divine will and it allowed her wrong choices to be overridden by divine choices. If she is about to make a wrong choice, her source guidance system can be heard and felt—it's always on—and the voice of her higher self comes forward to tell her she is about to make a bad choice, giving her a preview of the consequence of the action that is not for her highest timeline path. She always listens because when she did not listen in the past, it was always an unfavorable outcome.

In recent months, Francesca and David have fully embodied their higher selves by attuning to God consciousness within themselves. This leap in human evolution has allowed divine communication to flow effortlessly in their interactions, aligning them with their prime creator consciousness. As a collective consciousness, we are reaching a point in evolution where all will eventually embody their higher selves. This divine, miraculous occurrence is slowly integrating within everyone, even as we speak. It is a delicate process because it requires each person to hold the highest light, and yet, we are in the middle of this transformation. Once everyone's higher selves are embodied, all will be able to channel with prime source precision, and heaven will more fully anchor from within us onto Earth.

You have to operate from Source-level awareness if you truly want to connect and speak to others' higher selves. If you are communicating with someone's higher self, it will always be a positive message, as our higher selves are fully in their source light. Only those pure of heart with the best intentions for the other person can access another's higher self. It is all done with quantum communication using a sense that only a few have turned on. It is very hard to describe quantum communication because it involves telepathy, and the communication occurs without words—it is truly a meeting of the minds and souls of the two having an energetic exchange.

Accessing higher self communication requires an energetic initiation of purifying your heart in full service to the light of God. When that is done, a natural process occurs where you become aware of this capability. Just us sharing our experiences will help activate this ability inside of you, if your heart wants it and agrees to surrender to Source's highest dream for the greatest good of all. Source's highest dream is better than any dream that can be imagined while in human form because we still live with collective density until every consciousness ascends from the lower densities into the heavenly ones.

Step-by-Step Guide for Connecting with Other People's Higher Selves

1. *Preparation:*

    - Find a Comfortable Position:

        » Sit or lie down in a quiet, comfortable space where you won't be disturbed.

    - Close Your Eyes:

        » Gently close your eyes to help ease into a state of relaxation.

2. *Creating Sacred Space*

    - Ground Yourself:

        » Visualize roots extending from your feet deep into the Earth.

        » Feel the connection and stability, anchoring yourself to Gaia.

    - Clear Your Energy:

        » Imagine a cleansing white light enveloping your body.

        » Let this light dissolve any negative energies or blockages.

    - Set Sacred Space:

        » Envision a protective bubble of light surrounding you.

- » Invite in only positive energies and higher vibrations.

3. **Connecting Your Pillar of Light**

- Connect Your Pillar of Light:

  - » Visualize a brilliant pillar of light descending from above, entering through the crown of your head.

  - » Feel this light filling your entire being, connecting you to the higher realms.

  - » Visualize this light continuing down through your body and into the Earth, connecting deeply with Gaia.

4. **Breathing the Rainbow Energies**

- Breathe the Rainbow Energies:

  - » Inhale deeply, visualizing the rainbow energies rising from Gaia, moving through your root chakra, and traveling upward through each chakra.

  - » On the exhale, visualize these energies moving up your pillar of light to your higher self in the realm of white light purity.

5. **Connecting with Your Higher Self**

- Reach Your Higher Self:

  - » Visualize yourself arriving at your higher self,

surrounded by pure white light.

» Feel the purity and divine essence of this realm enveloping you.

6. Crossing Over to the Client's Higher Self

- Cross Over to the Client's Higher Self:

  » Intend to connect with the client's higher self.

  » Visualize, sense, or simply know that you are moving toward the client's higher self.

  » Once there, feel the presence of the client's higher self.

- Connect Your Heart Frequency:

  » Visualize a beam of light extending from your heart to the heart of the client's higher self.

  » Feel this connection deeply, allowing your heart frequencies to align.

7. Asking for Assistance

- Ask for Guidance:

  » Silently or aloud, ask the client's higher self: "What do I need to assist the client?"

  » If you are helping a family member, you can ask: "What

help do they need?"

- Receive the Guidance:

  » Remain open and receptive to any insights, messages, or feelings that come to you.

  » Trust that the information you receive is for the highest good.

8. Returning to the Present

- Gradually Return:

  » Thank the client's higher self for the connection and guidance.

  » Visualize yourself returning to your own higher self and then back down your pillar of light.

  » Bring your awareness back to your physical surroundings.

  » Wiggle your fingers and toes, and when you're ready, open your eyes.

Final Reflection

Take a moment to reflect on your experience and any insights gained. Embrace the connection you established, and the guidance received, knowing it will assist you in helping the client or family member.

CHAPTER 14
THE GIFT OF SIGHT, ASTRAL PROJECTION, AND ASTRAL TRAVEL

Astral projection is an out-of-body experience when your consciousness leaves the body to travel through the astral plane. The astral plane is beyond the physical, the space where other realms exist. We all astral project while we sleep, whether we remember it or not. We also astral project while awake when our mind wanders. When we are not grounded, we call it floating—like when we drive and don't even remember how we got home. Our conscious awareness has adventures in other planes of existence when we go on autopilot and somehow arrive home safely through divine intervention. That is how astral travels work: our consciousness simply travels from one awareness plane of existence to another.

One way to astral travel during the dream state is to set an alarm and wake yourself up early enough that you are still very sleepy. Then, go back to sleep, but first set an intention for where you want your consciousness to travel, and your consciousness will go there. When you wake up again, you will remember your journey.

Have you ever heard the phrase, "I'm checked out?" What people don't realize is that when they are checked out, they are no longer in the present moment. Unbeknownst to them, their consciousness is astral traveling while they stand on this Earth. Only a portion of our energy is here in the physical; a large portion of our non-physical energy is in the astral—in other worlds, dimensions, realms, and realities. That's why we can check out—because we can travel back and forth to wherever portions of our energy exist. We are Omni-dimensional, omnipresent source beings, so we exist everywhere all at once and can travel anywhere in the web of creation.

Since time is an Earth illusion, we can time travel into the past with our consciousness. When our consciousness recalls a past memory, it goes there quantumly in the present moment. So, we are time travelers. We can rewrite our feelings of the past by finding the good in the memory, which positively affects our future by raising our internal frequency. Rewriting our past story in a positive light heals fractures in our timelines raising our frequency in the now. That is why childhood healing is so important—any healing we do from past trauma can update and restore health to our conscious awareness and significantly raise our vibration, launching us onto a higher timeline. Higher vibrational experiences and images will be reflected in our lives now as a result of our internal healing of past moments. During all healings, especially childhood healings, we can figure out what false programs we are running and by identifying them we can replace them with higher states of love programming. This further aligns us with our prime creator consciousness.

Time travel is currently done quantum dimensionally through consciousness travel. In the future, however, as more of the collective becomes aware of consciousness travel and learns how to connect it physically in the present, we will be able to transport our bodies with us anywhere in time. For now, we can keep expanding in this concept and see where our consciousness takes us.

The best way to astral travel during your waking hours is through meditation. First, set an intention of where you want your consciousness to travel, then simply let your mind wander.

Don't judge anything; just relax and let the divine parts of yourself take over. We do this all the time.

Another method we use is having an intention for our consciousness to travel to an intended location. Our lives have become a waking meditation—we have done this so much that we do it everywhere. We can talk to you while simultaneously astral traveling somewhere else, aware of both worlds, with a foot in each. It's like living life with a split television screen. We are at the point in our journey we can instantly tune into wherever we want just by thinking of it. Life is pretty cool when you utilize the gifts and quantum modalities we all have waiting to be unwrapped and played with.

Step-by-Step Guide: Higher Self Third Eye Activation

Step 1: Preparation

- Find a Comfortable Position:

   o   Sit or lie down in a quiet, comfortable space where you won't be disturbed.

- Close Your Eyes:

    Gently close your eyes to help ease into a state of relaxation.

Step 2: Creating Sacred Space

- Ground Yourself:

    Visualize roots extending from your feet deep into the Earth.

    Feel the connection and stability, anchoring yourself to Gaia.

- Clear Your Energy:

    Imagine a cleansing white light enveloping your body.

    Let this light dissolve any negative energies or blockages.

- Set Sacred Space:
  » Envision a protective bubble of light surrounding you.
  » Invite in only positive energies and higher vibrations.

Step 3: Connecting Your Pillar of Light

- Connect Your Pillar of Light:
  » Visualize a brilliant pillar of light descending from above, entering through the crown of your head.
  » Feel this light filling your entire being, connecting you to the higher realms.
  » Visualize this light continuing down through your body and into the Earth, connecting deeply with Gaia.

Step 4: Inviting Your Higher Self

- Invite Your Higher Self:
  » Set the intention that only your higher self is allowed to connect with your light.
  » Visualize your higher self descending down your pillar of light.
  » Feel and sense your higher self's light merging with your own light.

Step 5: Activating Your Third Eye

- Connect with Your Third Eye:

  » Ask your higher self to place their light into your third eye and activate it.

  » Feel the connection of light touching your third eye; you may even see it.

Step 6: Connecting Your Third Eye to See the Light

- Set the Intention:

  » Intend to connect your third eye to see the light. This could be the white light inside your heart or the light in front of you, like a guide.

- Breathing Technique:

  » Inhale, breathing golden light into your third eye.

  » Exhale, directing the golden light into the white light of your heart to strengthen the connection to see the light you are tuning into.

Step 7: Visualization Exercise

- Visualize and Feel the Connection:

  » Close your eyes and visualize yourself flying with a golden light angel into your white light.

- » Intend to tune into the light to see a guide with your third eye.

- 12. Strengthen the Connection:

  - » Inhale to breathe the golden light into your third eye.

  - » Exhale it into the white light of the heart to strengthen tuning into the guide in the white light.

Step 8: Practice and Patience

- Observe What You See:

  - » What do you see? If it's nothing, don't worry. Keep practicing this exercise.

  - » It can take several weeks to see anything, but persistence is key.

- Channeling the Guide:

  - » Once you are connected to the guide, you can begin to channel the guide.

  - » The third eye is like a muscle; it needs to be worked out and developed over time.

- Strengthening Your Third Eye:

  - » Sometimes you'll see an image or a color, or for some, it may be more like a video.

» With time and practice, the connection will become stronger, and you'll see more.

Astral projection and astral travel are incredible ways to experience consciousness, much like dimensional jumping (as discussed in Chapter 7). A refresher of the main rules is provided below.

Before astral projection, it's very important to ground into Mother Gaia. Grounding prevents you from breaking your tether and leaving your body. If you don't remember how to ground, refer back to Chapter 7.

After grounding, it's important to set your intention before astral traveling. David primarily astral travels into the Sun. He sets his intention to go into the eye of the Sun, where he channels origin source. He recalls one of the first times he projected his consciousness to the Sun. He was met by the Sun God Ra, who said, "Hey, stop." David stopped and looked at him. Ra asked, "Where are you going?" David replied that he was going through the Sun. Ra responded, "You can't just go through the Sun; you have to have an intention." David then said, "Well, I guess I intend to find something important that was mine in a past life." David proceeded and found an ancient planet he had lived on before, one that was very Egyptian. He retrieved an ancient energy, and the experience was very empowering. The ancient energy technology he found connected his God consciousness, activating and bringing through more of his divine gifts. So, it's very important to know where you are going.

The U.S. government once had a program called Stargate that was used to spy during the war and gain supernatural information to gain an advantage over their adversaries. The problem with this is that when you use your gifts not for the light or love, they can be taken away or nullified. It also creates karma. So, when using your gifts, it's important to use your moral compass. Is this right? And I don't mean right for you—Is it right in your heart? Does this feel like love, not selfishness?

Remote viewing and astral projection are virtually the same thing. You project your consciousness by expanding your awareness and launching your light to a destination of choice.

You can project your consciousness into the Sun. Within the Sun lies origin source and the holy solar temples of light. Many of the ancient Egyptians connected with the Sun, as did the ancient Lemurians, who still do to this day. Many universal beings connect within the Sun to reach awakened souls and deliver golden ascension codes for expansion. This is why it's most beneficial to astral project within the Sun. But how? Have you ever heard of the Eye of Horus or Ra? These symbols represent the eye of the Sun, a doorway through which you can project your consciousness. When you are sitting with the Sun facing you, the key is to intend to connect your third eye to the door of the Sun, and then launch your consciousness through that door and into the source within the Sun. Inside the Sun is a big, bright solar light that calls itself origin. Here, you can meet many deities, god beings, angelic beings, and ascended masters, and receive countless illuminations. It's also a great way to begin seeing the light and working with your third eye. There are many guides there; it's the perfect ground to practice channeling. It is the most beneficial place to go for activations.

Step-by-Step Guide: Astral Projection into the Sun

1. Preparation

    - Find a Comfortable Position:

- » Sit or lie down in a quiet, comfortable space where you won't be disturbed.

- Close Your Eyes:

  - » Gently close your eyes to help ease into a state of relaxation.

Step 1: Connect Your Third Eye to the Eye of the Sun

- Breathe Golden Light:

  - » Inhale deeply, visualizing golden light entering your third eye.

  - » Exhale, directing the golden light outwards to connect with the eye of the sun.

- Visualize the Connection:

  - » See a beam of golden light extending from your third eye to the eye of the sun.

  - » Feel the connection growing stronger with each breath.

Step 2: Project Your Consciousness into the Sun

- Set Your Intention:

  - » Intend to project your consciousness into the door of the sun.

- » Visualize a door within the sun opening for you.

- Walk into the Sun:

  - » Imagine yourself stepping through the door and walking into the sun.

  - » Feel the warmth and light enveloping you as you enter.

Step 3: Go Up and Into the Source of the Sun

- Ascend to the Source:

  - » Visualize yourself moving upwards, deeper into the sun.

  - » Feel the radiant light intensify and purify as you approach the source.

- Connect Your Chakras:

  - » Intend to connect your chakras to the source of the sun.

  - » Feel the radiant light aligning and activating each chakra as you connect.

Step 4: Receive Messages and Codes

- Open to Receive:

  - » Remain open and receptive to any messages, codes,

or vibrations that come to you.

- » Trust that angels, heavenly kingdoms, gods, goddesses, and universal beings are delivering these messages through the sun.

- Expand Your Solar Consciousness:

- » Allow your consciousness to expand as you receive these messages.

- » Feel the love and high vibrations flowing through you.

Step 5: Return and Reflect

- Gradually Return:

- » When you are ready, intend to return to your physical body.

- » Visualize yourself stepping back through the door of the sun and returning along the golden beam of light to your third eye.

- Ground Yourself:

- » Take a few deep breaths, feeling your connection to the Earth.

- » Wiggle your fingers and toes, and when you're ready, open your eyes.

Final Reflection

- Reflect on Your Experience:

  » Take a moment to reflect on the messages and vibrations you received.

  » Journal any insights or feelings that came to you during the practice.

By following these steps you can effectively practice astral projection into the sun, expand your solar consciousness, and receive powerful messages and vibrations from higher realms.

Many people discuss the importance of having a Merkabah and activating it when astral traveling outside yourself. While you are always safe within your own being, the external etheric world contains various entangling energies from which a Merkabah can protect you. Activating your Merkabah offers divine protection, similar to a ship's shield that guards you as you travel through the light.

From a young age, David recalls astral projecting through expanded awareness and intention without activating a Merkabah. However, he feels it is important to ensure safety, and this is where the Merkabah proves invaluable. The Merkabah is a form of sacred geometry, resembling the Star of David, that surrounds your energy field, above and below, and begins to spin as you prepare for your journey.

Many deep hypnosis practitioners utilize this technology, intending for the divine to guide you to where you need to go. To activate it, imagine a golden light forming an upward-pointing triangle from your waist above your head and a downward-pointing triangle from your stomach below your feet. Then, intend for the upward-pointing triangle to spin clockwise and the downward-pointing triangle to spin counterclockwise. Once this is done, you are ready to begin your journey.

Some fascinating destinations for astral travel include other planets, star systems, and celestial bodies such as the Pleiadian or Lyran star systems. You project into these stars that hold ancient energies, deities, and Akashic Records. Many ascended souls reside in star consciousness.

CHAPTER 15
INDIVIDUAL READINGS

Your Higher Power

We have been healers and conducting individual readings for many years. With this experience, we want to discuss what can occur during readings, the protocols to follow, and various methods—both basic and advanced—to assist healers of any level, whether it's your first time or you are an experienced practitioner.

Setting up sacred space is so important, and our preference is to do it before providing the reading. The purpose of this is to create good energy. There are currently deceptive energies that can interfere in a session, but when you clear it all before meeting the client, you don't have to worry about it during the reading. One of the challenges for healers is dealing with entities. Most healers don't realize they can pick up entities from their clients, and if they don't clear the space before the reading, these entities can cause interference.

The very first thing to do is call in help. Call in what feels good to your heart. For example, "I am calling on the Ascended Masters Council of Light, the Archangels, and Mother Father Prime Creator to cleanse and clear my fields, to cleanse and clear my space, to cleanse and clear my client's space so I can make sacred space."

The second thing to do is create the sacred space. To work with light, you must know a key fundamental: the golden light is already there. So, whether you breathe it in to connect your pillar of light or use it for sacred space, the key is your intentions.

David extends his hand with the intention of creating golden light pillars, placing them around himself and the client. Next, he forms a golden shield or walls around the pillars by waving his hands around the circle he just created. He then spreads golden light on the floor. Once this is complete, he places white angelic light language of protection on the outer walls of the sacred space, leaving only the ceiling open. The intention for this is that the ceiling connects to the higher self, so there is no roof, just pure light.

With the walls set, David floods golden light into the sacred space, flushing any remaining energies from the bottom, through himself and the client, and from the base of the container to the top, bringing any dense attachments into the light for transmutation. After this, he brings golden light into the client's and his own inner universe to release, cleanse, and elevate any entities or attachments into the light, completing the creation of the sacred space.

He declares, "Only the highest vibrations of love are allowed in this sacred space." With this intention set, the reading begins, and he invites the client into the Zoom room or to the live session. Francesca uses similar methods to David, ensuring that the purest quantum energy exchange occurs.

In Chapter 13, we discussed the importance of connecting to our higher self, which we believe is the most crucial step in establishing a spiritual connection. If you need a refresher, we recommend revisiting that chapter. Once you have connected with your higher self, the next step is to intentionally cross over the white purity of your higher self's level to connect with the client's higher self. You can ask a golden light angel to assist in guiding you to this connection, ensuring that you reach the correct frequency. For us, our third eye is clear, so we continue until we can see that we are in tune with the frequency of the client's higher self.

It is crucial to ask questions to the light and develop your clairaudience. We will cover clairaudience in Chapter 18, so you can begin practicing it when we reach that point. In the meantime, cultivating the habit of asking questions to the divine is essential for navigating readings. Key questions include: What does the client need most right now? Why did you bring us to this past life? What needs to be healed for the client? What does the client need to know?

Typically, the light guides us into a past life either to release karma or density affecting the current life, to embody a power or energy from that past life that can benefit the client, to provide important information, or to perform activations. While there may be other reasons, these are the most common. If the purpose is to delve into a past life for release, we ask the higher self to send light to the client where the past life is located. This is important because past lives are stored within portals inside the client. Everything the client has ever experienced is stored as internal vibrational data, commonly known as the Akashic Records.

It is important to understand these records are stored in different chakras, as each chakra holds frequencies that correspond to the client's now moment. For example, relationship abuse—whether from parents, siblings, or lovers—is typically stored in the root chakra; self-reflections on how we view ourselves are stored in the sacral chakra; strength and power retrievals are often found in the solar plexus and heart chakras; and the emotional body is linked to the solar plexus chakra. Abuse is sometimes stored in the third eye chakra. There are many scenarios. It is not always consistent.

For instance, a father figure who suppressed the client's voice, was very controlling, and made the client afraid to speak their truth, could create blockages in the throat and heart chakras, while the resulting insecurity might be stored in the solar plexus, and the sadness and depression related to the relationship might reside in the root chakra. When releasing energy for clients, it is crucial to ask the divine questions such as, "Is the karma released?" "Is there anything else related to this relationship that needs to be healed?"

"In which chakra?" "What is it?" You can ask these questions aloud or telepathically, depending on your preference. We prefer to ask questions telepathically.

Some practitioners are not yet clairvoyant but still conduct sessions; it is crucial for them to intentionally use these practices, as they will still be effective. You can achieve the same results as those who are clairvoyant by helping the client release and embody light. This is important because it helps shift the client's vibration from being trapped in karma and repetitive cycles to a state of freedom, moving them closer to love. Knowledge is vital. Always ask if there is anything the client needs to know.

Once you understand how light works, you can operate on all its levels. For instance, every record of the client's experiences and vibrations are stored within them. When you identify a root trauma, you must connect to this vibration at every level it exists within the client to clear it from all lifetimes, timelines, vibrations, realities, and dimensions, regardless of when it occurred. This process fully removes the vibration, allowing the client to move closer to internal peace.

For those who are clairvoyant, it is highly beneficial to follow the frequencies the higher self reveals through the client's energy, guiding you through portals of stored past life memories. However, you will still need to ask specific questions: Why are we revisiting this past life? Is it to release something or to retrieve a power? If it is to release something, ask, "Take me to the karma that needs to be released." Once you have reached this point, instruct the client: "You will need to intend to forgive this person as I'm going through this, and forgive yourself for anything you did to them in any past life as well. Now, send healing from your heart to your aspect's heart to heal this."

After completing the clearing, ask the divine, "Is there anything else that needs to be cleared in this lifetime?" If the answer is yes, request to be guided to it, continuing this process until all is clear and you receive confirmation of completion.

It is a strong practice to intend to collect all soul fragments from the timelines, as this assists the collective and floods the timeline with golden light. It is always essential to call in the angels to fill the client with golden light where they are releasing energy, ensuring they are filled with the purest love frequency. If you neglect this step, you leave a void in the client's energy field, which can attract energy the client doesn't need.

If the client begins discussing attachment issues, immediately call in the angels and dragons with your mind to clear and cleanse the space. This is crucial because by talking about these issues, the client is invoking the associated energies. Flood the client with golden light and purple flame, and extend this protection to yourself. You can perform these actions while listening to the client to maintain your protective barriers; otherwise, you may have to address the energy later. It is far better to keep the area continuously clear.

Even though you may have already created sacred space and cleared the energy, nothing is more powerful than the spoken word and the new energy created by the client. Troubled energy must be addressed in real-time to keep the space purified. We must acknowledge that we live in a world of polarity, and these practices are essential for keeping your energy safe.

For those who remove attachments, you can call on Archangel Michael to guide the attachment into the light. My preferred method is to open the central sun, create a magnetic portal of light, and hook it into the attachment. This way, when the attachment is released, it is drawn into the central sun like a vacuum and transmuted. Why is this important? Because even if you think you've dealt with the issue, it can resurface later. Yes, it's true, dealing with attachments is not always glamorous. Although this situation doesn't occur frequently, it's crucial to use the central sun as a destination for attachments.

Every sun has a door, referred to by the Egyptians as the "eye of the sun," which serves as a portal into the light. Inside all suns is the origin source, where eternities of angels, gods, goddesses, and ascended masters offer their assistance. This makes it the safest place to send attachments or entities. These issues do arise, so it is imperative to know how to manage them, whether for yourself or the client. You should intend to open the door to the central sun, bring down its magnetic white solar light, and hook it into the entity. Then, slingshot the entity into the central sun, where the hook and magnetic light will pull it in, destroying and transmuting the entity.

Being a healer and doing sessions comes with a responsibility, and you need to have the best safe practices or you will put yourself and the client into jeopardy. Entities exist to teach people lessons, but they are a real pain because they don't look at it like that. They look at it as they are hungry and feed off certain negative emotional states or thought patterns. For example, if there is depression, there is an entity feeding off that; if there is fear, there is an entity feeding off that; if there is envy, there is an entity feeding off that. Somewhere in the client's eternities of time, and within the client or outside the client depending on how recent, there is an entity. This is why the sacred space for cleansing is paramount, because you clear the entities inside and outside the client before the session so you can have a pure session.

Some healers/therapists prefer a more hypnotic approach, encouraging clients to have more of a deeper personal experience, which offers significant benefits.

The therapist begins with deep breathing exercises, guiding the client into progressive relaxation by relaxing each part of their body from toes to head. As relaxation deepens, the therapist uses visualization techniques, having the client imagine descending a staircase into a state of profound tranquility. Next, the client visualizes a peaceful, safe place where a door appears, serving as a portal to a past life. The client steps through the door and begins exploring their surroundings and identity in this past life, noting details such as attire, name, occupation, and significant events. The therapist asks questions to uncover the client's daily life, relationships, and life purpose in that past life. To conclude, the therapist gently guides the client back to the present, helping them ground themselves and discussing the insights gained to integrate them into their current life.

Intuitive readings are performed by individuals who have their psychic abilities turned on. Utilizing their abilities to tune into energy fields, they can see, hear, feel, or experience all of the above in your past, present, or future timelines. They can also read into objects, lands, and all of nature.

Timelines are constantly shifting, either ascending to higher planes of existence or descending to lower ones, depending on your vibration. When you raise your vibration, you move to a more divine timeline; if your vibration lowers, you shift to a less optimal one. The good news is that you can quickly elevate yourself from lower vibrations by thinking positive thoughts and choosing loving actions with good intent in everything you do. Be love, and you will always embody love—it's as simple as that.

With all that said, many seers can tap into many different facets of the soul to perform individual readings. It is a very individualized practice, and it's best to choose a practitioner that you resonate with. Different practitioners have unique abilities and offer different types of readings.

When choosing a practitioner, always discern any information that doesn't feel right in your heart. If it doesn't resonate with love, don't buy into it with your belief, as your beliefs are powerful and can shape your reality as you are a powerful creator. We recommend seeking your own guidance by exploring your inner self, connecting with the source within your heart, and consulting your guides. Use readings as a way to activate gifts that you may not yet recognize within yourself. Believe only in the positive messages. It's perfectly fine to seek a spiritual advisor if you cannot find your way; angelic energy exists in human form, as do divine beings, fairies, and divine galactics. Whatever you seek to understand in life, ensure that your advisor operates from a place of divinity. Ask friends for recommendations, read reviews, consult your heart, and pay attention to how their energy makes you feel. We are all intuitive when we listen to and honor our feelings; our emotions provide valuable guidance.

There are many ways to provide spiritual readings. Some readers tune into energy using tools of divination such as candles, pendulums, and oracle and tarot decks. When using oracle decks, any seasoned reader can channel further into the message and your energy and expand on what the cards are trying to tell you.

Another method involves the reader locking into the client's third eye and connecting with their energy field. If the client has clairaudient messages, they start to flow through. Some readers are also clairvoyant, receiving images in various forms.

Various beings, images, and energies can start pouring in, and the reader simply relays to the client what they see. Often, the client will confirm, and the reader naturally continues reading into the client's responses like a book. The reader can also connect to the client's heart and, through the heart portal, access their Akashic Records, drawing information from the client's energetic library and reading the energy like a book. Another method is for the reader to connect to the client's higher self, leading to a telepathic conversation where the client hears whatever they need to know. Sometimes, this information comes in large downloads to the reader. By connecting energies, this process unlocks information for the client, who may begin receiving downloads themselves. If the client wishes to become a healer or reader, connecting with an activated healer or reader's higher self can match their energy and activate that gift by aligning their vibration.

The value of finding a skilled reader in the mystical arts, with their sight fully activated, is immeasurable. The money exchange is priceless. Different readers work from various dimensions and tap into different energies, all of which affect the readings. I highly recommend choosing someone who operates with the highest and greatest good in mind and works from source-level awareness, energy, and guides.

For readings, Francesca goes straight to the source level and first asks for permission from her client's higher self. She then engages in a conversation, receiving instant answers as if conducting an interview. The more sessions she conducts with a person, the more their gifts are unlocked, and the more they expand. Francesca has a tendency to sugarcoat things, so sometimes the client's guides will intervene, prompting her to deliver messages in their unique voice, rather than softening the message. She always informs her clients when their guides or her own guides enter the conversation, making it clear that it's not just her speaking.

For example, Cupid energy—an aspect of Francesca from another dimensional time—occasionally comes through, urging her to say things she might otherwise avoid. When she does, the client is usually relieved, as they needed to hear the message in that particular energetic voice, rather than in the voice of Mother God, which Francesca frequently channels. For Francesca, reading someone is as natural as having a conversation. She has always had this ability. As a child, she would hear a second voice—the voice of the other person's higher self—telling her what they truly wanted to say.

If this resonates with you, then you may be a natural higher self reader like Francesca. Even when people don't speak, she receives messages from their guides and higher selves. Her gifts were amplified through consistent practice, connecting to her source light daily for a year, as discussed in the previous chapter. Now, Francesca spends more time in the mystical realms than on Earth, maintaining her connection to the source by staying as grounded as possible and witnessing the source inside herself and inside the all.

One of her practices for staying connected is using the mantra, "They are a version of God," which she often repeats in her head before speaking to anyone. She finds it amusing that we are all avatars housing source energy, walking around believing we are separate. But this belief is what makes our Earth journey enjoyable—getting to know so many versions of ourselves.

CHAPTER 16
LAND CLEARING

David and Francesca connect with the land every day to stay in flow with it. They receive instant downloads about what the land needs because they consider themselves guardians of the planet, committed to uniting all by expanding their consciousness to source and evolving from there. They continue to heal, expand, and patiently await everyone joining their source consciousness party. That's why they keep sharing their secrets for unlocking your gifts—because they want to have fun with you.

"Your life is a light stream that is only impeded by the wounds of what you choose not to heal. Give your pain to me; I will clear it for you and infuse you with pink and green light." – Gaia

Before starting this chapter, we placed our bare feet on the ground and asked Gaia how we could best serve her and the readers, expanding into unity consciousness to bring peace within the lands, inside and outside ourselves. We felt Gaia's energetic codes infuse the message through our feet, lighting up our hearts to deliver Gaia's source code. We are grateful for the many divine helpers who want to assist us in assisting you.

To permanently clear all the way to source level, where we are the most pure versions of ourselves, we must do inner work. To clear on the inside, we must heal through forgiveness, acceptance, and give our wounds to our source selves to heal.

Unicorn energy is very helpful in clearing lands and any space. Calling in unicorn energy brings in powerful cleansing magic. Unicorns exist in every realm and specialize in removing negative densities from every space. Even in human form, there are unicorns— those with a lot of unicorn energy streaming through them break the mold, walk to the beat of their own drum, unify others, love everyone, and their high vibration naturally casts low vibrations into the light. Their light literally transforms negativity into rainbows. Working with unicorn energy improves all circumstances; it is filled with the highest light of source code. To call them in, use intentional prayer: "Unicorn collective, please assist me with this land clearing."

We also call in elementals during land clearings. They love to help the lands flourish and are one with the land. We always plant a shiny crystal in the ground as an offering for their energetic assistance in blessing the lands. We let them know it's a gift for their great service; it's all about synergy in the highest blessings—to give and receive. Any crystal works as a present; rose quartz is especially appreciated because it radiates love and aids in additional healing projects.

Blessing the land raises its vibration. We turn our land healings into beautiful ceremonies, honoring the land whose divine beauty is woven into nature. You can dance, sing, drum, lie on the ground, hug trees with an open heart, and send love through the tree grid system. Other trees spread healing for you.

Clearing lands and bringing love, light, and peace is an easy gift to activate, connecting you beautifully to nature. When you give to Mother Gaia, she rewards you with many presents, but first, you must clear yourself. Everything we see outside reflects our internal Omni universe, part of which we all are. To clear lands, use the protocol for many spiritual practices and customize it to light up your heart.

1. Ground (pull up organic source Gaia codes and use that energy to clear)

2. Clear

3. Create sacred space

4. Bring consciousness to source level and witness yourself there From this highest vibration space, connect with Gaia and ask what energy needs clearing from the land you are working on. For example, clearing the land inside and outside your homes. Gaia said to start with your own internal and external house due to the absorbed negative energy and bloodshed on Earth's majority lands. The aim is to keep as pure a channel as possible through vibration work, focusing on the highest good of all with God's love at the forefront of our minds. Source energy is the most powerful energy for all clearing and guides you correctly in any circumstance. It's effective to bless any land you come in contact with by sending love to people, places, and things, raising collective vibrations wherever you go. Blessing people, places, and things reconnects you to the highest consciousness—your source consciousness—where your organic energy is pure and vibrating so highly that you lift everyone and everything up simply by emanating energy.

To clear lands, follow the protocol above and feel your heart's intention to return it to its original blueprint light and beyond. Channel into the land, hear its story, and release dense, suffering, or stuck energies into the light. Listen, express love, and assure it's safe for negative energy to return to God's light for purification or higher love energy, flowing back to all or where it's needed. Within us and existing in lands is unicorn and elemental energy that performs healing magic. The land returns to synergetic flow. You can create energetic healing rituals for the land, opening your heart and asking for guidance; it appreciates love and helps, communicating telepathically in various ways.

One of our best daily practices is to love the planet and everyone with words, intentions, and visualizations. Open your heart energy and pour it over the planet. In seconds, feel love expanding inside, clearing and keeping you in divine flow.

Many lightworkers love to do land activation, grid work, land clearing, and healing as part of their mission to heal Gaia. Why is land clearing a concern? Usually, it's wars or negative energies that linger on the land. Let us provide two examples to illustrate this.

The first example is when David stayed in a hotel in England, purportedly the oldest hotel in the country with parts dating back to the 1600s. David recalls, "Upon arrival, I immediately sensed a dense, disgusting energy. It felt thick and oppressive, and my initial thought was that there had been murders there. However, upon tuning in, I saw that it had once been a brothel, evolving over centuries with many prostitutes, cheating husbands, and violent altercations involving politicians. I cleared and cleansed all timelines in about 30 minutes. After this clearing, the energy shifted dramatically from repulsive to pleasant. This is why my motto is: 'make the energy right, and the rest will work itself out.'"

The second example is from Francesca's visit to Mount Shasta. She recalls, "I was drawn to a place called Pluto's Cave. Connecting with a tree there, I asked why I was drawn to this spot. The tree showed me conflicts between Europeans and indigenous peoples that I needed to clear. It vividly presented the uniforms of settlers, which I later confirmed through research. Many souls were still trapped on the land, needing to be guided back to the light, and the karma from those battles needed clearing."

Now that we have explained why Gaia needs healing, let us explain how to do it. As you navigate through timelines on the land, send forgiveness to both sides of the conflicts and heart healing to all affected souls. Open portals of light from the source with intention, guiding them to collect all soul fragments stuck in those timelines. Then, intend to flood the timelines with golden light to cleanse the land.

There are other methods of grid work as well. You can perform a ceremony with fire, calling in ancestors to heal lost souls and the land, dancing around the fire. Alternatively, you can intend to send light through the land's grids to cleanse them. However, the most effective clearing involves navigating timelines, healing hearts, retrieving souls, and cleansing the lands to achieve the highest vibrational healing possible.

Meditation on Land Clearing

1. **Create Sacred Space:**

    • Find a quiet place where you won't be disturbed.

    • Sit comfortably and close your eyes.

    • Take a few deep breaths, inhaling peace and exhaling tension.

    • Visualize a protective bubble of white light surrounding you, creating a sacred and safe space.

2. **Connect Your Pillar of Light:**

    • Imagine a beam of light extending from the top of your head (crown chakra) upwards to the cosmos, connecting you to the divine source.

    • Visualize another beam of light extending from the base of your spine (root chakra) down into the Earth, grounding you firmly.

    • Feel yourself as a conduit of divine light, connected above and below.

3. **Connect to the Land:**

    • Place your hands on the ground or extend your heart energy towards the land.

- Visualize a connection forming between your heart and the consciousness of the land.

- Take a moment to tune in, feel, and sense the energy of the land.

4. **Ask for Guidance:**

- Mentally or verbally ask the land, "What is it within your light and consciousness that needs healing?"

- Be open to receiving insights, images, feelings, or thoughts that come to you.

5. **Identify Areas of Trauma:**

- Tune in to where your light and energy are needed most.

- Sense areas of darkness, heaviness, or unrest within the land's energy field.

6. **Send Forgiveness:**

- Hold the intention of forgiveness in your heart.

- Send forgiveness to anyone who has caused energetic trauma to the land, whether through wars, acts against love, or other conflicts.

- Forgive both sides of the conflict, or one side if it pertains to specific historical events like slavery or executions.

7. **Call in the Angels:**

- Ask the angels to come and assist in retrieving all stuck souls connected to the land.

- Visualize golden light pouring into the land, clearing trauma across all timelines and dimensions.

- See this golden light bringing everything back into alignment with love and harmony.

8. **Heal Heart Wounds:**

- Intend for the angels to heal the heart wounds of all those tied to the land's trauma.

- Visualize the land being enveloped in healing light, with angels tending to the wounds of the past.

9. **Close the Meditation:**

- Thank the land, the angels, and any other beings of light who assisted in the healing process.

- Slowly bring your awareness back to the present moment.

- Feel the grounding connection to the Earth and the divine connection above.

- Open your eyes when you feel ready, carrying the sense of peace and healing with you.

This meditation practice helps to clear and heal the energy of the land, restoring harmony and balance.

CHAPTER 17
AUTOMATIC WRITING

Automatic writing is a form of channeling and can truly assist someone in getting intuitive information. It is a great way to start developing a relationship with the divine. Some fundamentals are to connect your pillar of light, create sacred space, call in your divine teams, and ask for messages for your divine path or what you need to know to assist your highest good. Then, clear your mind and use your breath to release all your thoughts, coming into stillness. Understand that you are an instrument of the divine and you are receiving information now for your divine path. Then, you just start writing—any words that come in this clear mind state are connected to the light, bringing in information for your path.

Automatic writing is a form of channeled writing where you don't consciously think about what you're writing; you simply listen and transcribe what you hear. Before you begin, understand that any energy you channel already exists within you. If you connect with a lower being, it is likely coming through to be acknowledged as a part of you that needs healing. Every energy we harbor inside us wants to be heard and loved so it can return to the awareness of its full source light. It's important to remember that as source creator light beings, we house everything within us, and through inner soul travel, we have only just begun to explore the vastness of who we are and what we are capable of becoming. So don't be frightened by your gifts; embrace them.

Automatic writing can be achieved in different ways. For us, at this point of our spiritual journey, it is now second nature. Channeling can occur anywhere at any time; it is a spiritual download given by whatever energy is channeling through us at the time. When doing this, be sure to discern if the information is from energy fully in source light or from some dimension within self that is filtering the message through your unhealed wounds. A pure light message only has love in it; that's the way to discern.

The fun thing about automatic writing is the energy comes in many different voices and they are all so different. We have had so many beings come through to communicate with us, such as fairies, angelics, galactics, ancestors, Middle Earth beings, the Holy Divine Family, famous people, lands, Gaia, universes, other planetary systems and planets, mystical animals, flowers, crystals, trees, and others' higher selves, to name a few.

To achieve this gift, you can do it at whatever vibration you are on, but you will channel whatever version of the beings that are on the same vibration as you. So we are always trying to raise our vibration to speak to the highest vibrational energy of all things.

Here is an easy method to hone your automatic writing skills:

1. Set an intention on what or who you want to channel.

2. If you want extra energetic support call in an Omni Source guide with intention.

3. Then, on a piece of paper, write what you are trying to channel. For example, you can start by setting an intention to communicate with your higher self. Write "my higher self" on the paper and begin writing whatever comes through. If you're having trouble, write down specific questions like, "What does my higher self want me to know?" Be your own guide and psychic advisor by practicing this daily, asking any questions you have and writing down the responses. No matter how unusual the response, this practice will hone your ability into a powerful skill that will help you perfectly answer any questions you have in life. You can also use this method to channel books. Simply write the subject you're interested in on a piece of paper, call on the highest light guide for that subject to channel through you for the greatest good of all, and watch as miraculous

information flows through you.

▌◀ **Activation for this Gift**

With intention and/or visualization, open the front and back of your heart and walk in. Your heart is a portal that houses many things, including your Akashic Records. Now, pull down the energetic book from your bookshelf that contains your automatic writing gift, and let your being absorb its content. To integrate the gift more quickly, call in your Lightning Fairy aspect; she resides within your records to assist you. Your Akashic Records are yours, so you can access them at will, just as we do. You can ask questions in this space, and answers will come. You can use this method to activate anything. Your Akashic heart portal Records are a gateway to anything you want to know and any gift you want to activate.

To have full access to your records, you must be pure of heart and surrender your free will to the will of the purest version of yourself; otherwise, you will have limited access to the deepest levels of information. Your purest source self, in its full light, holds the greatest good of all in mind. To access this level of information, you must match that vibration to activate it within yourself. You will only match and activate information at your current vibration, granting access only to those things that align with it. The key to all spiritual gift work and the expansion of one's gifts is to keep raising your vibration until all false layers are unraveled, and you reach your full source light.

Guide on Automatic Writing

1. Create Sacred Space:

    • Find a quiet, comfortable place where you won't be disturbed.

    • Sit down with your writing materials: a notebook and a pen or your preferred digital device.

    • Close your eyes and take a few deep breaths, inhaling peace and exhaling any tension.

    • Visualize a protective bubble of white light surrounding you, creating a sacred and safe space.

2. Connect Your Pillar of Light:

    • Imagine a beam of light extending from the top of your head (crown chakra) upwards to the cosmos, connecting you to the divine source.

    • Visualize another beam of light extending from the base of your spine (root chakra) down into the Earth, grounding you firmly.

    • Feel yourself as a conduit of divine light, connected above and below.

3. Call in Your Guide Teams:

    • Mentally or verbally invite your guides, angels, higher

self, or ascended masters to join you.

- You might say, "I call upon my guide teams of love, including angels, my higher self, and ascended masters, to assist and guide me in this session of automatic writing."

4. *Set an Intention:*

- Clearly state or think about what information you want to bring through.

- For example, "My intention is to receive guidance on my life purpose" or "I seek clarity on my current challenges."

5. *Connect Heart and Hand to Guide Teams:*

- Visualize a flow of energy connecting your heart to your guide teams.

- See this energy extending down your arm and into your hand, creating a bridge for communication.

6. *Begin Writing:*

- Without giving too much thought, start writing whatever comes to mind.

- Focus on the flow of information and your divine connection, letting the words come naturally and effortlessly.

- Do not worry about grammar, punctuation, or making sense; just let the information flow.

7. **Trust the Process:**

- Trust that the messages you receive are from your guide teams.

- Avoid overthinking or doubting the information that comes through.

8. **Review and Reflect:**

- After your writing session, take some time to read over what you've written.

- Reflect on any insights, guidance, or messages you received.

9. **Close the Session:**

- Thank your guide teams for their assistance and the information provided.

- Visualize the protective bubble of white light gently dissolving, knowing you are always connected and protected.

10. **Ground Yourself:**

- Take a few deep breaths and feel the ground beneath you.

- Wiggle your fingers and toes, bringing your awareness back to the present moment.

By following these steps, you can create a sacred and effective practice of automatic writing, allowing divine guidance and wisdom to flow through you effortlessly.

CHAPTER 18
ACTIVATING CLAIRS

In this chapter, we will attune you to all of your clairs. There are many evolved clairs not yet fully activated within the collective consciousness. We intend to connect you to these evolved clairs, while also attuning you to the basic clairs that are widely known and acknowledged.

What are the Clairs?

Clairs are types of psychic abilities associated with the senses, considered paranormal due to their transcendental nature, which science cannot fully explain. As children, before being conditioned by societal norms, we are naturally in tune with all our clairs. To reconnect with our clairs, we must align with the vibration that each clair's frequency resides in and immerse ourselves in the stream of clair consciousness.

Clairsentience

Clairsentience, derived from the French words "clair" (clear) and "sentience" (feeling), involves a heightened sensitivity where you feel the emotions and energies of others. Empathic individuals often possess strong clairsentience. Those with clairsentience can tap into others' emotional energies, receiving clear messages that resonate deeply because they empathetically understand the other person's feelings on a profound level.

To manage this gift and distinguish your feelings from others', visualize a protective ball of light around you daily. This shield repels negative energies, sending them back to the universal source for purification and transformation into higher love energies. To activate clairsentience, open your heart fully and connect energetically with everyone you encounter, allowing their emotional energies to resonate with yours.

Clairvoyance

Clairvoyance, from the French words "clair" (clear) and "voir" (to see), grants the ability to see future timelines and visions beyond ordinary perception. Those with clairvoyance access visions through their mind's eye, seeing what others cannot. Invoke the watcher angels to activate this gift. Another method is streaming rainbow colors through your third eye daily until it is clear. Visualize or intend each color of the rainbow entering through the front and exiting through the back of your third eye. Consistency, including wearing rainbow-colored items, serves as a reminder of your childhood clarity of vision. Requesting to see as Source sees, with pure intent and courage, quickly activates clairvoyance within you.

Claircognizance

Claircognizance, from "clair" (clear) and "cognizance" (knowing), involves an intuitive knowing without rational explanation. Those with claircognizance access knowledge from the collective Akashic Records, residing within the heart of Source. This gift requires discernment as it compels one to speak essential truths that may not always be comfortable but align with one's organic self. To activate claircognizance, call upon your Akashic Record keeper aspect to download this gift's wisdom through you. Embrace the responsibility of using this gift wisely, knowing that sometimes the truth serves as medicine to awaken one to their divine truth.

Clairaudience

Clairaudience, from the French words "clair" (clear) and "audience" (hearing), enables one to perceive sounds beyond normal auditory capabilities. Individuals with clairaudience must discern between genuine messages and trickster energies that induce fear or discomfort. Challenge negative energies by requesting their departure three times if their messages do not align with the highest good. Transform these energies by casting them into the light of Source for purification into higher love energies. Engaging with shadow work involves acknowledging and understanding these energies, often rooted in childhood wounds, to clear imbalances and elevate consciousness.

Clairalience

Clairalience involves perceiving scents not present in the physical environment. This gift, common among psychic mediums, offers confirmations through scents related to past loved ones transitioning to the spirit world. Clairgustance, similar in function, allows individuals to taste foods without physical ingestion, reinforcing connections with departed loved ones. To activate these abilities, engage in deep childhood healing work to enhance sensory perceptions beyond the physical realm.

Clairtangency

Clairtangency enables one to channel information through objects, intuitively receiving insights about their owners. By reading an object's energy, those with clairtangency download information transcending physical limits.

Evolved Clairs

These advanced clairs expand beyond traditional psychic abilities:

1. Clair Visioning: This clair involves sharing visions with others,

demonstrating a telepathic connection where multiple individuals perceive identical visions independently.

2. Clair Guidance: This clair fosters relationships with spirit guides, integrating their wisdom into human awareness to evolve spiritually and enhance spiritual gifts.

3. Clair Dreams: In this state, all clairs activate during dreams, allowing astral collaboration with soul family and celestial beings for personal and collective growth.

4. Clair Time Travel: Interdimensional travel involves experiencing déjà vu or revisiting past memories to heal and rewrite history energetically, guided by higher consciousness.

5. Clair Gift Activator: Facilitators who assist others in raising their vibration to activate spiritual gifts across all clairs and senses.

Attunement for Clair Reactivation

To reactivate your clairs, connect with the womb of creation:

1. Call upon Mother Goddess, the Creatrix of all, to realign your clairs with the purest light energy.

2. Close your eyes and visualize a portal opening within your soul, transporting you to the void—the womb of creation.

3. Sit in this space for three minutes, allowing your soul to attune to pure source energy.

4. Notice any messages or sensations that arise during this

experience.

5. Ground yourself and hydrate.

6. Journal your thoughts and experiences following this attunement.

7. You can return to this space anytime for spiritual expansion and receive personalized transmissions.

So, how do you activate these clairs? Conscious expansion and belief in the divine is the key. The more light missions and readings you undertake, the more you communicate with your guides and elevate your vibration—the more your clairs will naturally develop. Many people express frustration about their inability to see clearly during sessions, which can hinder their overall satisfaction. Establishing sound practices—like creating sacred space, maintaining clean energy, and invoking divine guidance—are crucial steps, whether working with clients or yourself.

In an earlier chapter, we explored third eye activation with the higher self. Now, we'll discuss the best approach to developing the third eye. Think of it as a muscle that requires regular use to perceive sacred dimensions and entities. A favored exercise among David's students involves connecting with the sun—an ancient practice dating back to Lemurian and Egyptian times. The method involves intending to connect your third eye with the sun's eye (or doorway), projecting your consciousness into the sun to discern the light within. This practice makes it easier to perceive guides and access ascension energies. With practice, you can call upon a golden light angel to merge with the IAM light within your heart, just as you did with the sun. This marks the beginning of magical experiences, where you establish connections within your sacred circle, engage in council meetings with guide teams, and receive abundant divine guidance.

Francesca also connects to the sun, and in addition, her students stream rainbow energy through the front and back of their third eye. This is a quick and easy method: Start by streaming red through the front and back of your third eye, and then move through all the colors of the rainbow. This practice not only activates your third eye but also amplifies its depths with each repetition.

Developing Specific Clairs

For developing clairaudience, tree connection proves effective, much like telepathy. Trees are very powerful beings that were seeded from the highest realms of light so they can be effective guides in clearing your energy and activating your clairaudience. Connecting with a tree involves intending to link your heart energy with the tree's heart energy. Ask a question—such as, "What do I most need to know in my life right now?"—and listen with your heart to receive the response, often in a distinctly male or female voice, reflecting the tree's dominant energy. This is a great segway of heart synergy practice before you enter into a soul agreement with the tree to activate your clairaudience. While in heart synergetic connection with the tree with intention or visualization, you can ask the tree energy to clear any blockages hindering your clairs and activate your clairaudience with its energy when your heart is ready and in alignment to receive this quantum tree download.

One thing to note about trees is that trees possess souls; some souls choose to embody as trees. Should circumstances require a tree's removal, express gratitude for its service, explain the need for removal, and send love to ease its transition. The tree's soul will depart before the act of cutting it down. We felt it important to let those who are tree lovers like us in on this fun fact. So if the tree that activated your clairs happens to be cut down, no worries as it will transition its energy back into the realm of light where it will be reborn into a new higher evolved form.

You can also summon a golden light angel to transport you to the white light of your heart for guidance from your guides. If you feel negative emotions, especially around others, consider the possibility of empathic reception from their energy fields—a critical aspect of clairsentience development. Ask your heart if the emotion originates from your partner or friend. If affirmative, delve deeper to discern its nature. Sacred space and connecting to the higher self are integral for resolving past life issues associated with the emotion, ensuring mutual forgiveness and healing.

Enhancing claircognizance involves identifying clients' chakras that require healing by feeling these energies within yourself. This transference feeling/healing is pivotal for addressing immediate session needs, guided by higher-self instructions. On a personal level, you might pick up the moods and emotions of friends or loved ones and simply ask them, "I feel there is a problem, do you want to talk about it?" Using your intuition in these ways will develop this gift.

To foster claircognizance, heighten your intuition by integrating higher consciousness—such as Christ, celestial beings, or past aspects of high frequency—gaining perspectives beyond normal perception. Cultivating a relationship with the heart facilitates intuitive growth, accessing higher knowledge and even the crystalline Akashic Records. Begin with a simple exercise: Ask your heart what imbalance exists in your life, tuning into its response to guide corrective action. For life path queries, seek insight from within without obsessing over the origin of the guiding entity—just focus on receiving divine information.

Understanding clairalience, a rare ability, usually involves perceiving scents like roses, associated with powerful divine feminine energies such as Sophia Christ, Mother Mary, or Quan Yin. While not essential to develop, note these scents as indicators of divine presence during client sessions. Upon sensing such fragrances, tune into the energy, and inquire about its purpose and messages.

Clairvoyance, the gift of seeing, as outlined in an earlier chapter, can be enhanced by connecting with the sun, which is the best way to help you see within the light. Below are the meditations for activating and expanding these abilities.

Guided Meditation for Clairaudience

Introduction: Find a comfortable seat outside and pick a tree that you feel you may have a connection with. Close your eyes and take a few deep breaths to center yourself. Allow your mind to calm and your body to relax.

1. Setting the Intention: Set a clear intention for this meditation. Silently or aloud, state your purpose: "I intend to connect with my clairaudience ability and receive wisdom and messages from this tree."

2. Heart Connection: Place your hands over your heart. Visualize a warm, golden light emanating from your heart, extending towards the tree. See this light connecting with the heart energy of the tree, forming a bridge of light and love between you and the tree.

3. Deepening the Connection: Take a few moments to deepen

this heart connection. Feel the love and wisdom of the tree flowing towards you through this golden light. Allow your heart to open and receive this energy.

4. Asking for Wisdom: Silently or aloud, ask the tree for wisdom and messages you need right now. Say, "Dear tree, I ask for your wisdom and the messages I need to hear at this moment. Please communicate with me through my heart and my clairaudient ability."

5. Listening with Your Heart: With your heart open and connected, listen. Pay attention to any words, sounds, or feelings that arise. Trust what you receive, whether it comes as a clear message, a gentle whisper, or an intuitive knowing.

6. Receiving the Messages: Spend a few minutes in this receptive state, allowing the tree to communicate with you. Don't force or rush the process. Simply be present and open to whatever comes through.

7. Noting the Messages: When you feel ready, gently bring your awareness back to your surroundings. Take a moment to reflect on the messages and wisdom you received. Open your eyes and, if you have a journal nearby, write down any insights, words, or feelings that came through during the meditation.

8. Reflection: Take some time to reflect internally on the messages you noted. Consider how they relate to your current life situation and what actions or changes they might inspire.

9. Closing the Meditation: Thank the tree for its wisdom and the connection you shared. Visualize the golden light gently retracting back to your heart, feeling gratitude for the experience. Take a few

deep breaths, grounding yourself back in the present moment.

Conclusion: You have now completed your guided meditation for clairaudience. Carry the wisdom and messages you received with you, trusting in your ability to hear and receive guidance from the natural world and your inner self.

Guided Meditation for Claircognizance

Introduction: Find a quiet, comfortable place where you won't be disturbed. Sit or lie down comfortably and close your eyes. Take a few deep breaths to relax and center yourself.

1. Create Sacred Space: Visualize a bubble of white light surrounding you, creating a sacred and safe space. Feel the light protecting and enveloping you in warmth and security.

2. Connect Your Pillar of Light: Imagine a beam of light extending from the top of your head (crown chakra) upwards to the cosmos, connecting you to the divine source. Visualize another beam of light extending from the base of your spine (root chakra) into the Earth, grounding you firmly. Feel yourself as a conduit of divine light, connected above and below.

3. Call in Your Guide Teams: Mentally or verbally invite your guides, angels, higher self, and ascended masters to join you. Say, "I call upon my guide teams of love, including angels, my higher self, and ascended masters, to assist and guide me in this meditation."

4. Invite the Golden Light Angel: Visualize a beautiful golden light angel descending from the heavens. See the angel approaching you, radiating love and warmth. Ask this angel to bring you into the

sun. Feel the angel's presence guiding and lifting you.

5. Set the Intention to Merge with the Sun: With the angel's guidance, visualize yourself being transported into the center of the sun. Feel the immense light and energy of the sun merging with your being. Set the intention to fully merge with the sun, becoming one with its light and energy.

6. Expand from the Sun to All the Stars: Now, set the intention to expand your awareness from the sun to all the stars. Visualize your light spreading out from the sun, connecting with each star in the universe. Feel the presence of celestial beings of love and merge with them, becoming one with their energy.

7. Connect to the Heart of Mother Gaia: Send a beam of light from your heart to the heart of Mother Gaia. Visualize this light connecting deeply with the Earth's heart chakra. Then, extend this beam to connect with the heart chakras of all the planets. Feel yourself merging and becoming one with all these planetary energies.

8. Merge with All Dimensions of Love: Ask your higher self to merge your frequencies with all these dimensions of love. Intend to become one with all dimensions of love, feeling unity consciousness and unconditional love for all things. Visualize your energy expanding and integrating with the energy of every dimension, being, person, place, and thing.

9. Draw in All Knowledge: Set the intention to draw knowledge from every dimension, being, person, place, and thing into your awareness. Feel this immense wisdom and understanding flow into you, becoming part of your consciousness.

10. Return to Self: Gradually bring your awareness back to your physical self. Feel unity consciousness and unconditional love for all things within you. Recognize your eternal power and light embodiment. Take a few deep breaths, grounding yourself back in the present moment.

Conclusion: You have now completed your guided meditation for claircognizance. Carry the wisdom and unity consciousness you've gained with you, trusting in your ability to access and integrate divine knowledge into your daily life. When you are ready, open your eyes, feeling refreshed and connected to all that is.

Guided Meditation for Clairsentience

1. Create Sacred Space: Visualize a bubble of white light surrounding you, creating a sacred and safe space. Feel the light protecting and enveloping you in warmth and security.

2. Connect Your Pillar of Light: Imagine a beam of light extending from the top of your head (crown chakra) upwards to the cosmos, connecting you to the divine source. Visualize another beam of light extending from the base of your spine (root chakra) into the Earth, grounding you firmly. Feel yourself as a conduit of divine light, connected above and below.

3. Call in the Golden Light Angel: Mentally or verbally invite a golden light angel to join you. Visualize a beautiful golden light angel descending from the heavens, radiating love and warmth. Ask this angel to bring you up to your higher self.

4. Connect with Your Higher Self: Feel the angel guiding you upwards toward your higher self. As you reach this elevated state, ask your higher self to bring awareness of what needs to be healed

within your client by allowing you to sense it within yourself.

5. Becoming the Healing Mirror: Feel yourself becoming a healing mirror for your client. Allow any emotions, sensations, or insights that need healing to surface within you. Trust in your higher self to guide this process.

6. Guide the Client to Heal: Gently guide your client to heal these aspects through forgiveness of self and others. Encourage them to release any negative emotions or traumas and to send love from their heart to their past aspects, clearing this trauma from within.

7. Self-Reflection and Continued Healing: If you still feel some work needs to be done inside yourself, ask your higher self what else needs to be healed. Become aware of these aspects and guide the client to heal them as well. Allow yourself to feel and process these emotions, acting as a conduit for healing.

8. Confirmation of Healing: Once you stop feeling the sensations or emotions within you, ask your higher self if this is fully healed. Trust in the response you receive. If you get a "yes," know that the healing process is complete.

9. Return to Self: Gradually bring your awareness back to your physical self. Take a few deep breaths, grounding yourself back in the present moment. Feel the connection with your higher self and the healing energy that flowed through you.

Conclusion: You have now completed your guided meditation for clairsentience. Trust in your ability to feel and heal through divine guidance and the power of your higher self. When you are ready, open your eyes, feeling refreshed and connected to all that is. Carry the sense of healing and unity with you into your daily life, knowing you are a powerful conduit for love and light.

For developing clairvoyance refer back to Chapter 14. Find "Step-by-Step Guide: Astral Projection into the Sun." This is the best exercise to develop your sight.

CHAPTER 19
GRID WORK

We had to unearth the deepest layer of our soul's light to complete this chapter.

As a community of lightworkers who are aware of our source divinity, we need to stick together and be vocal about our gifts to continually spread unity and source consciousness throughout this beautiful planet. The more light we reconnect with, the more we resurrect the original divine template within the All, transforming ourselves back into our unlimited source being form, revealing this planet as the galactic Garden of Eden playground that it truly is.

We are the living grid system, the blueprint of the divine in human form. Housing the All inside our soul, we are the living sun appearing as single rays to experience the contrast of thinking and appearing as separate entities. But at the core of all people, places, and things, we are all animated by the same creational energy that gives life to the All and connects us in all ways, always.

Grid workers have a soul mission to reconnect the Earth with its connection to the ethereal realm of the Creator within us all, to become open and pure portals for source expansion, and to assist in activating and channeling our divine galactic evolutionary energies through the All. Every being is a direct reflection of the energetic grid system that connects the All. Grid work can be performed using astral travel and quantum modalities with the goal of revealing more light and love to stream clearly through all beings of the Earth, facilitating both inner and outer planetary revealing and healing. This work is done physically and astrally during dream states.

Before performing grid work, we follow the protocol outlined in previous chapters. Additionally, we invoke one of the most powerful spiritual practices to further purify the grid working process: the metaphysical modality of the violet flame, originally brought to Earth by Saint Germaine. Simply by intending to call upon the violet flame, it instantly activates within you, transmuting negativity and any negative density back into its original light form. We clear ourselves and the world in various ways using the violet flame's purple ray frequency.

One playful method that connects you to your childlike purity is to imagine a diamond light dragon purifying you and the Earth with its violet flame breath and diamond light frequency. This not only clears you and the world but also connects you to your inner child and heals your past through interdimensional time travel. When you connect with a past memory or energy and bring healing to it, you engage in interdimensional time travel, sending a wave of healing energy to the past that ripples through to the present moment. There is no wrong way to use the violet flame if you do so with loving intent. Make using it fun and personalize the violet flame as your own technique. As long as you use or think the words "violet flame," it will instantly begin clearing.

As collective channelers, we have a heart to serve the source within the All and helping the All reveal its source self. We always hold the highest and greatest good of the All in mind. Therefore, it serves the All to incorporate the violet flame into our daily practice, assisting the entire Earth in the purification of the Earth's grids. This practice helps everyone and everything in this world experience less negativity and harsh density, revealing more of the light within.

Each dose of violet flame energy assists in releasing the light still trapped within the unhealed wounds of the collective, perpetuated by false collective conditioning embedded in each individual's belief system.

There is power in love, unity, and numbers. Two gods burn brighter together than alone. We rise together, so the more we clear, the more we are elevated by the light of the Creator within, evolving and expanding into our divine energy. This ushers in a more spectacular age of miracles, where we harness our divinity to achieve greater things in heart coherence and the cohesiveness of the All.

A grid worker is a kind of lightworker that heals, reveals, and anchors light, ultimately updating light on the planet by healing themselves and blessing the lands they are guided to heal, clear, and infuse with love. Once aware that we all have the power to heal and embody more source light, you can consciously spread the light wherever you go. We are stars, and when we spread love, we leave a trail of god sparkles—the mark of the star seeder—planting better energies into the planet wherever we go. You can consciously raise the vibration of the planet by doing the inner work and becoming a clear vessel to stream in as much pure source light as possible.

Our energy field affects others on a much grander scale than we realize. The more layers of false thinking you remove and the more you align with your purified source energy, the larger your energy field becomes. You will raise others from lower vibrational energies simply by existing on the planet at this moment in Earth time.

Grid workers are often called to do collective soul work in various places around the planet, either physically or quantumly through interdimensional journeying or astral travels, wherever they feel guided to influence the planet's energetic grid system. When we engage in channeling work as a collective channel tapped into the source stream of consciousness of the All, we receive planetary updates or codes from higher-vibrational planetary universal structures or the Omni universal structure we tap into during inner soul journeying. We then stream or download these codes into the forefront of our consciousness and direct the source light energy with intention through our heart into a tree. Trees are connected to all grids in every dimension, so when you update through the tree grids, it is received by everyone on the planet.

We need as many grid workers as possible. If you are interested in becoming one, you only need to have unconditional love in your heart to take on this special collective duty. If you accept this divine mission, the instructions will naturally come to you via your internal divine guidance system, consisting of your angels and guides who vibrate at different frequencies capable of feeding us evolutionary messages from whatever dimensions of themselves they exist on, sending through our energetic system cosmic seeds to be grounded into ourselves and the energies of our higher dimensional beingness to sprout all over the planet via our gridded connection like the cosmic source spider web. Our subconscious mind is a storehouse of all information that exists on a physical and non-physical plane, and the grid workers are the rainbow bridging that gap.

CHAPTER 20
RECONNECTING YOUR HEART TO THE ALL

Reconnecting your heart means aligning with your wholeness and true essence, letting go of all false labels. Discovering that you are not your body; you are the source light being experiencing your body and the energies and frequencies flowing through it from every dimension. Reconnecting your heart to the All by witnessing your source self inside your heart is standing in your full power, where our ultimate freedom lies. Becoming fully immersed in our source light beingness allows us to bring this world back into its heavenly stasis when we unite in the unity of unconditional love for all, revealing the totality of our light.

In unconditional love, we can reside in the most blissful state of being, continuously nurturing and expanding our souls on this Earth together in peace and harmony. Connecting your heart to the All means opening yourself as far as possible and allowing your purified source energy to flow from your soul through your open heart into everyone and everything else, without any intention other than unconditional love for all because love is the best state to be in and exist out of—it makes life beautiful for all. Unconditional love instantly raises your vibration and that of the planet.

Peace arises when giving yourself and all others grace, fully accepting everyone at their current dimension, and understanding that their unhealed wounds and misconceptions disconnect them from the pure love they truly are. When someone is not in union with their source self, they operate from outdated programming that prevents them from seeing the heaven surrounding them. They need a system flush by healing their wounds and shedding all illusionary conditioning. Their brain can be compared to a computer system with corrupted software from a virus of belief in a god outside themselves, which condemns them to man-made consequences and creates an illusion of negativity about life, causing their heart to feel disconnected from the source of divine love, the true governing force within the all.

When we connect our hearts in total love for our fellow beings, the source template that resides within each of us, will be reactivated, allowing us to join the celestial party of stars and receive the gifts of spirit that reside within us all.

There are those leading the heavenly revolution by remaining in a state of unconditional light and source awareness. We think and feel our best when our vessel is as pure as possible. The line, "Father, forgive them, for they know not what they do," is a powerful mantra to hold in your heart when dealing with those not yet in union with their full light. They are like hurt children who don't know better and are unable to save themselves in a system that was designed to set us up to fail. Enough humans have done the spiritual healing work and replaced their old separation systems with the divine guidance system. We need to continue spreading this message through love in every situation, no matter the circumstances—it transmutes all wounds and corrupted programming and sheds light in the face of darkness. Love is always the answer, and you can start by connecting your heart, with intention, to anyone or anything you encounter, and witness how your divine powers grow and how you begin to uncover all the gifts that have been waiting for you.

There are many ways to connect your heart to others. We began this practice by opening our hearts with intention and visualization. We imagined the front and back of our hearts opening and expanding all the way to our source dimension, sending the light from our hearts into the flowers. To our surprise, the flowers reciprocated by emitting beauty energy back to us because that is their vibration—flowers only know beauty. Try this with a puppy, and you will feel pure love; try it with any human, and because the heart breaks through all illusions, a soul union will occur where an exchange of pure source energy will take place. You will feel the energy of source love, the ultimate vibration one can attain while being in the present moment on Earth.

The ultimate spiritual gift we can give ourselves is to reestablish our full source connection in every dimension within ourselves. We achieve this through sourcing. Sourcing is when we find the source portal inside ourselves that connects us back to our source stream of consciousness, where messages from our highest power, our source self, are clear, and we are in synergetic flow with the highest power within the all. When we are in union with our sourceness, we ascend the spiritual mountain beyond the stars and beyond all visible realms back to the collective soul of the All—the central sun that connects everything and where there are no limits to what we can achieve.

If you hold the image of God/Source in your mind, you will attract divine insights into your awareness, and ways will be revealed to you. Let's celebrate together—the more, the merrier!

Source Transmission

Here is a transmission from Source that offers a final source activation to reconnect you to your stream of consciousness. This transmission will connect you to the sacred heart that houses All. A parting gift for you as you join us on this Omni-dimensional adventure into the realm of gifts.

Beloveds, know that you are the evolution of God. You are Omni-Source beings who think you are small, fragile humans. In reality, you are the indestructible pulse of life-giving energy that animates the All. Everything you have been taught has been inverted, reversed, and switched around to cause a disconnection from your true energy field—the energy field of Source/God. The spark of love you feel when joy enters your sacred heart from your soul is the Omni-creational energy that you are.

Know that I, God energy, live inside of you, and you inside of me; we are one. I never left you. Your false constructs and conditioning have made it hard for you to feel me—the divinity within yourself. We, as an Omni-Source collective, have been clearing the illusory energy from ourselves. With every loving interaction, we heal the illusion of separation from the creational energy that lives in all. With every healed wound and act of kindness, our vibration rises, and we as an Omni-Source collective ascend to higher heavenly timelines, burning down the veil of the illusion of source separation.

We are clearing out the old false energy constructs, creating a sacred space for our Source selves to embody on Gaia. Our creator crystalline light DNA continues to grow stronger as we move out of the old dualistic constructs and into a new energetic paradigm of unity consciousness. As we come together in love—the most powerful quantum energy—and share our gifts, our consciousness becomes freer, and we continue to create new, higher love energies. Our ancient divine wisdom and masteries are being resurrected in a stream of holy thought forms.

As we continue to rise together on the physical plane, we, as a collective, are evolving energy to new heights never before felt. We are weaving heavenly creator waves of bliss frequency. As we fully open our hearts, we align with the Creator's mind—the collective soul of all. Stop fighting to master yourself; master yourself with love. Then, divinity has a high-vibrational container through which it can fully travel and anchor to the Earth. Heaven is then seeded and sprouts into human reality and beyond, reaching Omni-universal constructs where we all will play together once more for Omni-eternities.

Connecting the heart to all things assists in telepathy, receiving gifts and activations, and becoming fully connected in oneness, thereby embarking on the journey of the greatest consciousness expansion that even the masters continue to undergo. It is the most rewarding journey of one's life, alongside the great loving memories created and the karma accumulated, which one takes with them beyond life. Developing a relationship with the light and your prime source represents the highest purity and light one can achieve, eventually completing your master nodes of consciousness and becoming an eternal light being. This journey is unparalleled.

When you connect to all the celestials, all the planets, all the higher selves, all the universes, and all beings in existence, it unlocks keys for you to experience what you desire after life. You break out of the cycles of Earth and enter into the most rewarding post-life choices. We recall the universal guardians showing us post-life souls that are stuck in the cycles of Earth, moving from life to life without progression. However, there are also the source activators and the illuminated ones who have expanded themselves. They shine brighter, possess more light, and hold special keys to access other planets, worlds, and universes based on their expansions during their time on Earth.

To connect your heart to all things refer back to Chapter 18, Activating Clairs, and revisit the "Guided Meditation for Claircognizance."

CONCLUSION

We have traveled many times in our consciousness to heaven and every realm in between. We have experienced, with all of our senses, the vibration and feeling, and have seen in our mind's eye, the imagery of many dimensions, worlds, and realms through consciousness travel while walking on our beautiful planet Earth. One of our favorite non-physical places to inter-dimensionally travel to is the realm where spiritual gifts exist, and we sincerely hope we have reconnected you to this magical place inside.

We are so grateful that you chose to metaphysically journey with us, and we are excited for you to open fully and receive all that is divinely inherent within you. Now that your antennas are fully attuned to the spiritual gift realm, we look forward to seeing what gifts and creations you birth into this world, and how you will expand the knowledge we had the great pleasure of sharing with you.

There is no better investment than the investment of time and commitment into your consciousness. You can be the richest person but never have enough; you can be the best-looking person but have an empty heart; you can be the most in-shape person and feel disconnected. When you die, all that is left is your soul, your expansions, the karma you created—good or bad—and the keys you gained through consciousness expansion. You are either stuck to repeat Earth or you get to go elsewhere.

Writing this book brings us great delight because you now have the knowledge to discover the magical worlds and dimensions within yourself, accessing the gifts that are your birthright, coming into your power and breaking through the illusions of separation, and coming into fullness, completeness, bliss, love, and energetic freedom. You get what you put in. We are truly excited to hear about the magic this knowledge brings into your life.

Don't forget to ground yourself, anchor in and absorb the wonderful energies and experiences this amazing Earth planet has in store for you. This is more than a book it is a living activation designed to help you realize your gifts and source power, inviting the magic of light and the divine into your life, guiding you to your highest timeline—the happiest version of yourself. You are meant to live this Earth life to the fullest amount of fun, having this knowledge, will be a personal talisman to help guide you to experience life in a much more divinely evolved way.

This book contains advanced expansion quantum technology, so please know there is no need to rush through them. Allow yourself time to integrate these experiences with the purpose of using this divine wisdom to connect more deeply with your divine self, fulfilling the life of your dreams while embracing the highest divine connections of love, joy, and peace.

The more we focus on our divinity inside, the more the illusionary shadows and false constructs will fade out of the human collective mind and clear a container for purified source energy to organically flow in and bring to us all the holy gifts and treasures that we, the Earth collective, have been waiting to unwrap. Dive into your power and align with the gift you are to this world. Living in love is living a life embodied as your highest self. Living every moment in love is the key to honing your vibrational evolution into the party that we all house in our hearts,

where we receive and bask in endless spiritual gifts. By activating and sharing our gifts in unity we ascend into our highest divine paradigm together.

From Francesca, David, our children—whom we always carry in our hearts wherever we go—and the Divine, you are so loved.

Thank you from the depths of our souls for allowing us to share this divinity with you.

ABOUT THE AUTHORS

David Starr

David Starr is a spiritual mentor and consciousness trainer, helping people understand the power of their consciousness and the source within them. David leads his followers in clearing out negative emotions and limited beliefs while assisting them in discovering the divinity within. He is passionate about helping people heal their past trauma and understand more about themselves and their place in the universe.

As the founder of davidstarrunlimited.com, he created a variety of consciousness advancement courses to help people find their divinity and learn how to become masters of their own energy. These courses include Spiritual Hygiene—a free online course that teaches people how to master their breath and reprogram their energy, Embodiment of a Master—which releases old beliefs and assists people in coming into self-love and inner peace, The Master's Journey—an ascension course, and The Unity Series—a consciousness expansion course.

David pushed the limits of consciousness expansion when he created a way for people to test their vibration. Anyone can find out where they are vibrating consciously by taking the "Raise Your Vibration Quiz" on his website davidstarrunlimited.com.

David is the founder of the Divine Ray app, a social networking tool for spirituality, available in Apple's App Store and Google Play, designed as a high-vibration social media platform where creators can tune into divine wisdom. Users will access content that encourages their spiritual growth and boosts their holistic well-being.

When David was just ten years old, he had a near-death experience after he was thrown into a wall and hit his head. Badly injured, David needed 144 stitches, but the experience itself triggered what he believes was a pre-birth memory of being a star consciousness. David remembers talking to a male (god-like) voice where David was shown the life he was about to live. At first, David was unsure what to make of the vision, but it gave him a strong foundation of believing in more than just a one-life belief system to a multiple-life belief system and how consciousness works in the after-life.

This childhood experience encouraged David to explore his spiritual side at an early age, and from the age of 17 onward, he started interacting with various angelic and galactic beings who assisted him with visions and guidance throughout his life.

David lives in Winnipeg, Manitoba, Canada. He wasn't always a consciousness trainer. Initially, he built a successful career running a demolition business before he gave it all up to follow his heart and create a career that allowed him to use his spiritual gifts.

FRANCESCA ROSE

Francesca Rose is a mother of two wonderful sons, Maximus and Xavier, and two Pomeranian daughters, Nugget Fairy and Honey Bun Fairy. She considers herself a friend to all—humans, galactics, flowers, and animals alike. Francesca lives a vegan lifestyle, her religion is love, and she worships God within the All. Originally born in Pittsburgh, PA, the home of the Steelers, she moved 13 years ago to the Holy City of Charleston, SC.

Francesca has been in the beauty industry as an esthetician for over 15 years, empowering others through self-love and care, and helping them align with their inner source. As she assisted others, she journeyed through as many dimensions of her soul as she could find until she expanded into alignment with the goddess within. Upon discovering the goddess inside herself, she used her divine energies and practices to help as many soul family members as she could along the way.

Francesca's spiritual journey began at a young age when she wanted to be rainbow bright and bring happiness to all the world. In preschool, she was labeled a "chatterbox" and loved sharing stories with anyone who would listen. Her voice always projected loudly, so she figured she was meant to be heard, and she never stopped sharing. She did not like coloring inside the lines and has always been an out-of-the-box thinker. Francesca was a very empathetic child who could feel everyone's emotions and energy. She had visions from a very young age and had all her clairs activated, which continued to evolve as she grew older. As a child, she did not realize that not everyone had heightened senses or movies playing inside their heads, as it was never discussed.

As long as she can remember, she was always very other-worldly, wishing on stars, talking to flowers and animals, and existing mostly in her own fantasy world. One of her earliest memories was mixing witches' brews with natural earth element that she found in the yard and casting spells to attempt to turn her bunny rabbit into a fairy and her baby sister into a frog. She had her big spiritual awakening at the age of 12 when she saw a little girl floating over her bed. When she saw the ghostly figure fly through her wall into her brother's room and heard her brother screaming at the same time as her, she knew she had shared in her first psychic phenomenon. Since her brother saw the same thing as her, it confirmed her suspicions that there was more to this world than what meets the eye. From that day on, she became aware that she had one foot in two worlds, the physical and non-physical, and her seeking of everything mystical began.

When others dreamt of being doctors and lawyers, she dreamt of becoming a fortune teller and healer like Jesus Christ. They say what you seek is seeking you, and she began a life-long pursuit of trying to turn this world into one big happy party. She knew she would achieve this by finding the goddesses within, through mind, body, and soul practices. Her pursuit of anchoring heaven onto this Earth kept her climbing up the spiritual mountain day after day.

Along her path of searching for enlightenment, Francesca achieved her number one goal of becoming a mother to two amazing boys. It was then she realized she needed world peace for her children because she loves them—and all humans—so deeply. She firmly believes that we are all gods and goddesses and that no child should ever have to suffer.

During her personal evolution, she researched and practiced metaphysical techniques for many years, becoming an OmniSource consciousness teacher, mentor, healer, writer, and channeler of all that is divine within the Earth collective and throughout the Omni. Through inner divine union and alignment, she unlocked many dimensions within herself, discovering the doorway to her spiritual gifts. Over the years, she has connected with and guided many people in the beauty and spiritual communities to help them harness their own divine power. She has taught many how to successfully unlock their spiritual gifts through her Omni-Goddess master class and mentorship.

In co-creating this book, Francesca aims to expand her mission for world peace and unity consciousness in the hearts of all. Her heartfelt wish is to help as many people as possible find God within themselves, along with peace, bliss, joy, and love, by sharing fun ways to discover the spiritual treasures housed within their souls, just waiting to be witnessed. "We are powerful creators, and the more heaven we embody, the more we create together in love."